electronic
discourse

SUNY Series in Computer Mediated Communication
Teresa M. Harrison and Timothy Stephen
Editors

electronic discourse

*linguistic individuals
in virtual space*

Boyd H. Davis
and Jeutonne P. Brewer

State University of
New York Press

Published by
State University of New York Press, Albany

For information, address State University of New York Press,
State University Plaza, Albany, NY 12246

Marketing by Nancy Farrell
Production by Bernadine Dawes

Library of Congress Cataloging-in-Publication Data

Davis, Boyd H.
    Electronic discourse : linguistic individuals in virtual space /
Boyd H. Davis and Jeutonne P. Brewer.
        p.   cm. — (SUNY series in computer-mediated communication)
    Includes bibliographical references (p.) and index.
    ISBN 0-7914-3475-3. — ISBN 0-7914-3476-1 (pbk.)
    1. Discourse analysis—Data processing.   I. Brewer, Jeutonne,
1939– .   II. Title.   III. Series.
P302.3.D38   1997
401'.41'0285—dc21   97-11131
                                                           CIP

1 2 3 4 5 6 7 8 9 10

Contents

Preface

In 1989 we created a mainframe computer conference presenting primary-source newspaper texts on the Civil Rights Sit-Ins of the 1960s for our classes in linguistics, which were located on two university campuses. During the next four years, we replicated the conferences and expanded the participation between the two real-world settings.

This book looks at what student writers do with language, and how they do it, when they participate in electronic conferences. It seeks to ground discussions of how to assess electronic discourse and the impact of technology on communication by a description and analysis of what this group of users actually did in and with the medium. We found that individual writers drew on their own idiolects to influence the form and nature of electronic discourse, adapting their own tacit knowledge of conversational strategies and written discourse to the new medium in order to create a real, if temporary, community.

The students came to the conferences with an obligation to participate, but without expertise in using the mainframe conferencing software, VAXNotes, which was new to the computer systems when the conferences were devised. Like many conferencing programs, VAXNotes allows the exchange of messages within a closed group on a particular topic, for particular purposes, which frequently focuses some sort of collaborative work. Conferencing software archives all messages so that they are immediately retrievable by topic, author, or date; VAXNotes messages are title-driven as well. That is, the writer creates a title after writing a message instead of creating a subject-descriptor before writing. Titles in the Sit-Ins

VAXNotes conferences, which the software arranged as subtopics, were both the writer's summary and the reader's first clue to the content of a student-generated message.

On the level playing field of a group assignment, which stipulated a minimum number of replies, students set about the task of investigating the new world of a computer conference. Neither the conferencing interaction nor their temporary discourse community, united by a common task and a general topic, existed before they created them. Both went out of existence after they had completed their discussion of the issues they had discovered and the issues they had introduced. This study analyzes the techniques these groups of students used to establish tacit norms for their exchange of ideas, opinions, and feelings, the ways they conferred authority upon themselves and recognized it in others, and the ways they encultured each other in the town meeting they used as a forum to discuss socially sensitive issues as presented and represented by language use in the sixties as well as the nineties.

Many linguists have written extensively on the basic linguistic concepts that contribute to language shaped by a wide range of new technologies. Our study examines the particular manifestations of the general principles in the language of a particular group with a particular purpose as they wrote their comments in computer conferences. Each chapter begins with a discussion of such principles, which may already be familiar to linguists.

Outline of chapters

Chapter 1, "Beginning to look at electronic discourse," introduces electronic discourse as one form of electronic communication. Electronic discourse must be described and analyzed before a decision can be made to classify it as a new genre or a register of the language. Because electronic discourse is like *spoken* language in some ways and like *written* language in other ways, the researcher must examine this new form of language use in terms of individual as well as group characteristics. The corpus for this study consists of three conferences involving slightly different social situations, which were conducted over three consecutive semesters. Their virtual setting changed over the years of conference replication, from the Stand Alone conference, which included a single class on a single campus, to the Transparent conference, which included students from both campuses in the same conference. Our analysis of this corpus, roughly 340 pages of conventionally printed running text, includes study of the full corpus, the individual conferences, and the writings by individual students and by groups of students.

Chapter 2, "Context and contact in electronic discourse," gives an overview of the ways student writers dealt with the new, the unreal, and the unknown as they created discourse spaces for themselves in a community that came into being electronically. Their sense of audience varied with their sense of where they stood in relation to the events they read and wrote about. The conventions they used, the ways they accommodated each other, and the ways they repeated and emulated each other often placed them in positions like those of speakers of different languages in contact. They moved back and forth between more formal and less formal styles of language, signaled by word choice, by sentence structure, or by persuasive technique. Their shifts in style and variation of discourse features allowed them to continue their interaction and signal different purposes to their audience. These shifts were enabled by multiple layered repetition and emulation. The final artifact of the conference, the text left behind after the writers had departed, displays ways the writers chimed into each other's statements.

Chapter 3, "Entering the conferences: Challenges of time and space," describes the situations and settings, both physical and virtual, of the conferences, as well as characteristics of the participants who moved among them. Students brought a media-based construct of the sixties to the conferences, since most had been infants or young children when the Sit-Ins began. The two campuses had different settings through which the students could access the conference: one group used microcomputers in a central campus computer lab; the other group appropriated terminals housed in a variety of buildings. Both groups found their sense of time disoriented in the virtual setting of the conference, which asked them to examine the language use and events from the sixties in the context of the nineties. Each group found their expectations about genres of newspaper writing and about objectivity and detachment to be confounded by primary-source texts waiting for them in the conference.

Chapter 4, "Titles: Form and function in electric discourse," investigates the ways titles signal interaction among student writers. Here we look at conventions of direct and indirect address, signals of personalized response or disclosure to accompany the title, and preview an elaborate game with titles that signaled community-formation in a conference that linked students from both campuses. Synchronic snapshots of particular conference interactions show how titles played a role in the social situation of the electronic conference and how titling conventions shifted when students' frames of reference changed. "Guardedness" shows how students first established, then guarded, their territory, their spatial equivalent to establishing authority and self-legitimization. These shifts characterize conference discourse.

Chapter 5, "Defining the territory," looks more closely at features the students used in developing their two prevalent styles and ways of establishing authority for their roles and rights to speak about issues. Repetition of words and phrases and emulation of larger patterns of discourse were the primary means for signaling assent or dissent, involvement or detachment, from peer-generated writings. We examine how their use of pronouns shifted time and space, review the presence and absence of some gender-cues in the writings, and present examples of how student writings established credibility for the writers and indirectly addressed the other writings in the conferences.

Chapter 6, "Taking a stance: Text, self, and other," looks at lexical repetition and syntactic cues that characterize student shifts in style or register. We look more closely at selected writings to see how the writer signaled with lexical, syntactic, or discourse signals when shifting. Students qualified the force of their assertions to each other by drawing on features of modality to suggest their attitudes or opinions. An examination of form and functions leads us to look at clusterings of modal verbs as they co-occur with public or private verbs, qualifiers, and lexical variation. The patternings of clusters in two different conferences show how students shaded the ways they explained what they meant in the context of two different kinds of audience: one restricted to their own individual campus (Stand Alone conference) and one that linked both campuses (Transparent conference).

Chapter 7, "Aspects of emulation," examines features of topic popularity and the rhythms of response patterns that developed in individual topics and a conference as a whole, in order to see how these factors might impact the ways students emulated each others' discourse strategies. We found changes of frame and focus as students adapted their own preferences from conversational interaction. Such as notions of adjacency-pairing, or moved into writing language about language. Such adaptations showed student writers accommodating their assumptions of audience in various ways throughout their narrative responses.

Chapter 8, "Emulating a strategy: The rhetorical question," looks at a single feature. We examine how students adapted the convention of rhetorical questioning from oral speech in order to enculturate each other into acceptable wordings, and how they intertwined rhetorical questions with direct and indirect address to establish common ground or consensus for sharing and giving information. The ways students used the construction of the rhetorical question as a strategy proved to be a major difference between the Transparent conference and the Stand Alone conference.

Acknowledgments

We thank here Mikki Burgess, Mark Caskie, Jacob Molyneux, and Brent Yugen, who appear under different names in this text, for their assistance in the analysis of the corpus. We thank as well the several hundred students participating in the conferences since 1989. The names of all student writers in the conferences have been changed to protect their identities, unless otherwise noted, although students gave us permission to study and report on their writing. We continue to learn from them.

We thank the computer center staff on both campuses for helping us work out problems in setting up the conferences on new computers with new software. Special thanks go to Bob Blackmun of the University of North Carolina at Charlotte and Marlene Pratto of the University of North Carolina at Greensboro for their interest in the use of computers in the humanities.

We are grateful to Guy Bailey, Barbara Johnstone, Connie Eble, Ralf Thiede, and the anonymous readers of this manuscript, whose helpful comments guided us. We hold them in no way responsible for the views we present in this study.

We dedicate this book to Dick Davis and Chris Brewer, both of whom made their own contributions to this project.

1://A first look at electronic discourse

On defining electronic discourse

Electronic discourse is one form of interactive electronic communication. In this study, we reserve the term for the two-directional texts in which one person using a keyboard writes language that appears on the sender's monitor and is transmitted to the monitor of a recipient, who responds by keyboard. The recipient may actually be a single individual or a group, large or small, of receivers. Like any other way that humans use language for interaction and communicative purposes, electronic discourse is multifaceted and complex. Since the textual artifact resulting from electronic discourse is written language, both language in general and written forms of language are included in its study. Inasmuch as electronic discourse involves interaction among people, the text implies something about the variety of social interactions among its composers.

Electronic discourse is not a surrogate for language, such as whistle or drum systems, but a different context for its use. It is the interaction of that context with language that is interesting. While people have invented or evolved a series of conventions within different types of electronic discourse, it is probably premature to claim that it is a new genre within the repertoire of a language's performance possibilities. Instead, in this study, we begin with a basic question: Is there anything that might differentiate the ways people use language in electronic discourse from those in, for example, an exchange of signals by flags, a series of postcards, letters to newspapers, or successive sections of an epistolary novel? Before deciding whether to classify electronic discourse in any

1

particular language as a genre or a register of that language, we must begin with preliminary description and analysis of what electronic discourse seems to be or do, and what people choose to do with it. To do this, we draw on the field of discourse analysis: first, because the various approaches within discourse analysis are suitable for the task of describing and analyzing text, and second, because discourse analysis is, in itself, multidisciplinary. The kinds of questions we ask of the text and of ourselves are being asked by scholars in several disciplines.

The term *electronic discourse* focuses on how individuals use language to exchange ideas rather than on the medium or channel by which they transfer and deliver their messages. Using this term, as opposed to the term *computer-mediated communication*, emphasized our focus on language above the sentence—on language as utterances (Schiffrin 1994), whether written or spoken. Writing is often seen as space-bound, static, and permanent, whereas speaking is viewed as time-bound, dynamic, transient. Electronic communication, written on keyboards and read on computer screens, has many characteristics of both speaking and writing. Like telephone conversations, it is transmitted by a technology that replaces face-to-face communication, in the case of the telephone conversation with voices speaking and in the case of electronic discourse with images on a screen. Like letters, electronic discourse is supported by a delivery system that replaces face-to-face communication with writing that stands in place of voices. As a consequence, electronic discourse is writing that very often reads as if it were being spoken—that is, as if the sender were writing talking.

Writing that reads like conversation

Electronic conference discourse exchanged by university students participating in mainframe conferences as part of a course is multiparty interaction through extemporaneous, rapidly written keyboard composition. It reads like and to a certain extent acts like conversation. However, the discourse cannot be analyzed only or primarily by the methods used for the analysis of conversation because—aside from being unspoken—electronic conference discourse is asynchronic. It thus has a different kind of immediacy of feedback or response. That is, interactivity is delayed: the time between the creation of text between sender and responder may range anywhere from several seconds to several weeks, or even longer, depending on the length of time that the conference is available to its participants.

Electronic discourse also differs from face-to-face communication in turn taking. Turn taking is constrained for electronic conference discourse, both by time and by the computer software, which also delineates boundaries between utterances and archives each written utterance as received. Hence the interruptions and overlaps so characteristic of converstion are not possible. Electronic discourse can alter or rearrange the sequential ordering of conversation's adjacency pairs, which speakers and analysts use to track the sequence of conversational interactions or discern topical or thematic shifts. For example, Lee is reading and responding to Carter's note received on a Tuesday at 3 P.M., and pauses before saving the message within the program. On the same day and at the same time, Biff composes a message in response both to Cane's from the preceding Friday and to Carter's. It is completed on Tuesday at 3:01 so that it is saved by the software before Lee's. The messages, then, are distributed as coming in the order of Cane, Carter, Biff, Lee. Thus, their chronological distribution will not represent the actual timing of the utterance exchanges. In electronic conference discourse, interactivity draws on two time frames: that of the sender and that of the responder. Since conferences typically involve multiple people, the two time frames may intersect but are not necessarily immediate in their interaction.

Electronic conference discourse is like conversation in that it presents a number of performance features generally characteristic of in process or in situ communicative events and behaviors, such as repetition, direct address, disfluencies, and markers of personal involvement. These features include syntactic and lexical items on which Biber (1988) performs multivariate analysis in order to derive dimensions characterizing genres of written and spoken text.

The features may also be graphic. Wilkins (1991) notes the use in electronic mail discussion lists of all-capital letters, the creation of emoticons, the use of punctuation to signal humor or irony or a sense of intimacy. In her collection of multiparty conversation on a conferencing network for an electronic communications utility over a three-months period, Wilkins (1991) observed that what kept the conversation flowing was not references by name or number or established conversational sequences. Instead "the conversational topic was maintained through lexical repetition, synonyms and shared cultural knowledge" (63).

Speaking and writing: Biber's dimensions

Lexical repetition and variation is probably the most immediately noticeable feature in electronic mail and in electronic conference discourse. Biber's series of analyses of variation across spoken and written forms of languages has shown that "linguistic variation in any language is too complex to be analyzed in terms of any single dimension" (1988: 22). His goal was not to set up or to confirm an absolute distinction between spoken and written language. Rather, it was to "specify the multidimensional relations among the many different types of speech and writing in English" (25). He identified four notions that are useful in discussing both speech and writing— integration, fragmentation, involvement, and detachment (43). He used these notions to identify six dimensions of variation (expressed as two opposing poles on a continuum), which characterize genres in both speaking and writing. These dimensions collapse co-occurrences of features that serve to typify or characterize different genres of discourse as being *involved* in nature as opposed to *informational*; *narrative* as opposed to *nonnarrative*; *explicit* as opposed to *situation-dependent*; offering *overt expression of persuasion*; *abstract* as opposed to *nonabstract* in terms of information; and presenting *on-line informational elaboration*. The application of Biber's dimensions can be extended to the study of electronic discourse.

According to Biber, integration ("the way in which a large amount of information is packed into relatively few words") is present in writing, but not generally in speech, which "cannot be highly integrated because it is produced and comprehended on-line" (43). Here, *on-line* refers to the constraints of time and immediacy accompanying speech. Careful word choice, in other words, is expected in written discourse, but does not characterize most kinds of speech situations. Electronic messaging in real time, or very brief synchronous interactive electronic communication, is more like informal speech situations. Because of its *integration*, electronic conference writing, though extemporaneous, is more like written discourse.

Fragmentation, shown by such features as clauses connected by "and" as opposed to subordinating conjunctions, characterizes text produced under severe time constraints, such as a typical speech interaction. *Involvement* is suggested by linguistic features of interaction that refer directly to the recipient of the text. It contrasts with *detachment*, often marked by agentless passives and nominalizations, which characterizes situations that are not two-way interactions. Like other forms of speech and writing, electronic discourse may be analyzed for these functions.

Is it sufficient to consider electronic discourse only as writing? It is both possible and instructive to analyze a corpus of electronic conference discourse as notes—longer than a comment, shorter than an essay—that all deal with one or more aspects of a topic and which cluster into several very general themes and probably some fairly distinct narrative patterns. In that sense, we could reconstruct and study the text of the interaction as if it were a thematically organized sonnet sequence, perhaps, or a series of commentaries glossing a series of specific texts, as with midrash.

Problems arise, however, with the order in which different entries in electronic discourse can be read and analyzed. The electronic conference sustains an event of language contact. Multiple texts, and through them, their writers, are in contact in a variety of ways. The entries in electronic conference discourse can be arranged in chronological order for the whole conference, but that order jumbles topical or thematic threads of discussion and omits the role of the individual text or writer. Entries can be arranged by the order of entries keyed to one specific text or topic, but that order jumbles the chronology of the whole, though it can present an array by each topic. Entries can also be arranged in terms of the writings by each writer in order to track connections across topic or time. One order facilitates looking at the group through synchronic arrangement of contiguous texts. Another order facilitates looking at change in individual writings over time. Reading the artifact of an electronic conference—the text remaining after the interactive performance of its writers and readers—is not a straightforward task. In this study, we examine features presented by the group, by the topic, and by the individual, turning the kaleidoscope of discourse in order to look at the role played by the individual within the group.

Biber's analyses of a wide range of spoken and written varieties of English have demonstrated that "there is no single, absolute difference between speech and writing in English; rather there are several dimensions of variation, and particular types of speech and writing are more or less similar with respect to each dimension" (1988: 199). Therefore, we cannot look only at speech or only at writing in order to characterize electronic discourse, because the two share many characteristics. Electronic discourse, an interesting and important example of language use and text, is different from the conventional sense of both spoken and written language.

Multidisciplinary perspectives

Scholars in several disciplines, such as sociology, anthropology, rhetoric, psychology, composition theory, and folklore, currently ask similar questions and often present complementary perspectives about writing, social situations, and conversation, drawing on insights from earlier work by linguists and anthropologists. Analysis of electronic discourse is keyed to how one thinks about everyday conversation or narrative, or about the ways that special kinds of writing and special features of ordinary speaking are interrelated.

Scholars from several disciplines have begun to apply the findings of linguists who examine contemporary spoken and written language and their relationships to each other (see, for example, Chafe 1986; Chafe and Danielewicz 1987; Tannen 1990; Biber 1988). Schiffrin (1994) and Johnstone (1996) have called for multidisciplinary perspectives on the study of discourse. Scholars in allied disciplines endorse the interdisciplinary examination of communicative discourse in general and electronic communication specifically (Baym 1995; Collot and Belmore 1993; Eldred and Hawisher 1995; Ferrara, Brunner, and Whittemore 1991). From the perspective of communications studies, Rice (1982, 1987), Galegher, Kraut, and Egido (1990), Dunlop and Kling (1991), and Foulger (1990) emphasize different aspects of collaborative work, usually within organizations or businesses, in order to see if and how electronic discourse supports and even improves the work, the product, or different kinds of interactions within a group or team. Hiltz (1984), Sproull and Kiesler (1991), and McGrath (1990) have assessed electronic interactive communication in organizations and businesses (see Finholt and Sproull 1990). Theories underlying the process of collaboration in writing tasks have been discussed in the fields of composition and rhetoric, particularly in terms of notions of social construction; that research is reviewed from a variety of perspectives by Lanham (1992), Tuman (1992a), Faigley (1986), Bolter (1991), Duin and Hansen (1994), and Selfe and Meyer (1991). Studies of teaching applications involving interactive electronic communication, whether within a single classroom or spread out across a county, a country, or several continents, include Harasim (1990), Hawisher and LeBlanc (1992), Harrison and Stephen (1996b), Baldwin (1996), and Kaye (1992). Studies of setting (Foulger 1990), gender (Herring 1993), and other aspects of social organization discerned in or effected by electronic discourse (Eldred and Hawisher 1995) have begun to influence research, particularly as scholars note the interdisciplinary nature of such efforts.

In order to determine where and how electronic language fit Biber's dimensions, Collot and Belmore analyzed a corpus of electronic messages that were organized into nine subject areas—chitchat, current events, science, science fiction, finance, film and music, photo and cooking, medical, and sports (1992:45). They found the features characterizing electronic language to be most like those in the dimensions for two genres Biber had studied: public interviews and personal and professional letters. While they identified situational features affecting language use, Collot and Belmore were not able to determine the extent to which the situational features affected the "overall linguistic configuration of Electronic Language" or the "relationship of the participants to the text" (Collot and Belmore 1993: 53). In her study of a Usenet newsgroup that discussed daytime soap operas, Baym concluded that the "complex and dynamic process" involved in the development of patterns for identity, norms, and communication point to the need for more "naturalistic, ethnographic, and microanalytic research" in order to "refine our understanding of both influences and outcomes" (1995: 161).

Studies like these point to the need to look at electronic discourse from the microlevel as well as the macrolevel. Whether people are using computer networks to interact and communicate in "real time" (synchronous) as on the telephone or in delayed time (asynchronous) as with letters, whether their computers are side by side, in the next room, in the same town, or a continent away, they are using computers for the purpose of communicating with each other. One focus on these various uses can be the channel being used—that is, the way the networks, the computers, the hardware and software, and the connections support the act of communication. Another focus can be the context in which the communication takes place. This study focuses on the latter in order to examine how people adapt their approaches to and their ways of communicating in different contexts. Electronic discourse is discourse that takes place in those contexts. What the individual participants do with language in order to discuss issues and create a community is the basis for understanding the various levels of electronic discourse. How the "linguistic individual" (Johnstone 1996) relates to the text and adapts to the electronic context provides the key to understanding the linguistic and social features of electronic discourse. The fabric of electronic discourse is language; the weavers of that fabric are the individual participants.

Selected approaches to discourse analysis

Just as there is no longest sentence, there is also no longest stretch of discourse, which is generally considered to be language beyond the sentence. There is no single theoretical approach to analyzing discourse. As Deborah Tannen notes (1989: 6–7), discourse analysis may seem sprawling, even "heterogeneous," because "it does not grow out of a single discipline . . . it is by nature interdisciplinary." In *The Linguistic Individual*, Barbara Johnstone (1996: 22) reminds us that discourse analysis can also be defined, following Coulthard, as "situated speech or, following Brown and Yule, as "language in use." Johnstone frames her study of the individual's consistency and idiosyncrasy, undertaken "to show how paying attention to individual voice helps in understanding language" (4) by calling for "the kind of language study I find most compelling, the work A.L. Becker . . . calls 'modern philology.' As was the traditional philology that gave rise to modern linguistics, modern philology is centered on particular texts" (4). Johnstone calls on scholars to look, then, not only at speakers seen as a group or at an idealized system, but also particular utterances and at approaches that "locate language and dialect in the individual's creative choices for how to talk and understand" (13). Her approach to discourse analysis has the goal of understanding language through understanding the text. Speaker-centered linguistics, a linguistics "once again willing" to draw on philology as "the close reading of texts considered to have historical or literary value" (180) will find that "one's text or texts, rather than one's theory, tends to be the source of discipline" (24).

Looking at text, and specifically at written text, is one of the concerns of discourse analysis. According to Tannen, discourse analysis is a term that "describes the object of the study" and which developed "in order to make legitimate types of analysis of types of language that do not fit into the established subfields of linguistics, more narrowly focused, which had come to be regarded by many as synonymous with the name of the discipline, and to encompass work in other disciplines that also study language"(1989:6–8). In her survey of the different approaches to the analysis of discourse, Schiffrin (1994) identifies six key methodologies, each drawn from different areas of linguistics. Each of these methodologies views language in its social context from a slightly different perspective. Speech act analysis "focuses upon knowledge of underlying conditions for production and interpretation of acts through words" (6). Pragmatics analyzes "speaker meaning at the level of utterances" (9). Interactional sociolinguistics examines "how language is situated in particular circumstances of social life and on how it adds (or reflects) different types of meaning . . . and structure . . . to those circumstances" (7). Ethnography of communication analyzes "the structures and functions of communicating that organize the use of language in speech situations, events, and acts" (185). Conversation analysis looks at how "members of a society produce a sense of social order" (232; see 9–10). While interactional sociolinguistics, ethnography of communication, and conversational analysis assume a language-as-interaction model, variation analysis assumes a language-as-code model (385; see 405) to examine the distribution and variation of forms across text types (331).

In this study, we draw on insights and perspectives from inter-actional and variationist sociolinguistics, the ethnography of com-munication, and historical linguistics, in whose bosom philology still nestles: "in Old Irish, or Hittite, or Vedic Sanskrit, or Indo-European studies, everyone does both linguistics and philology on a daily basis, and it's no big deal" (Watkins 1990: 22). As Watkins reminded the Linguistic Society of America in his presidential ad-dress of 1989, both philology and pragmatics are "the study of the meaning of language forms as these depend on the linkage of signs to the context in which they occur" and that "good comparatists like a Saussure, a Wackernagel or a Delbrück moved freely and effort-lessly between diachrony and synchrony" (1989:785). The exami-nation of electronic discourse involves the analyst with both planes as well as with both older and newer approaches to discourse.

Suzanne Fleischmann's (1990) comments about texts in Old French are, we think, particularly appropriate to the study of elec-tronic discourse with its features of both oral and written language:

> As a linguistically oriented philologist, I am convinced that many of the disconcerting properties of medieval vernacular texts—their extraordinary parataxis, mystery particles, conspicu-ous anaphora and repetitions, "proleptic" topicalizations, and jarring alternations of tenses, to cite but a few—can find more satisying explanations if we first of all acknowledge the extent to which our texts structure information the way a spoken language does, and then proceed to the linguistic literature that explores the pragmatic underpinning of parallel phenomena in naturally occurring discourse. (Fleischmann 1990: 23)

As linguists interested in synchronic and diachronic aspects of lan-guage as they occur in text and discourse, and thus in philology, we adapt to the study of electronic discourse Ochs's (1990: 289) defi-nition of discourse as "a set of norms, preferences and expectations relating language to context, which speaker-hearers draw on and modify in producing and making sense out of language in context." Our primary goal throughout the study is to reconstruct the elec-tronic conference text and to identify and describe features impor-tant to its structure. "Structure, or regularity, comes out of discourse and is shaped by discourse as much as it shapes discourse in an on-going process" (Hopper 1987: 142).

Schiffrin's (1994: 39) principles for discourse analysis assume that discourse arises "not as a collection of decontextualized units of language structure but as a collection of inherently contextualized units of language use." Discourse analysis is empirical—that is, it is sequential, distributional, and predictive. It is more than the sequence of its linguistic units, in that "forms and meanings work together with social and cultural meanings, and interpretive frameworks." It assumes that discourse is interactive, sequentially situated, and is "guided by relationships among speaker intentions . . . conventionalized strategies for making intentions recognizable . . . the meanings and functions of linguistic forms within their emerging contexts . . . the sequential context of other utterances . . . the properties of the discourse mode. . . . the social context . . . [and] a cultural framework of beliefs and actions" (316). Our examination of electronic discourse is sequential and distributional. For example, we look at sequences of utterances as units and as sequences within texts, at how individuals shift styles keyed to their own intentions, and at how they develop conventions and appropriate strategies from each other. We describe the computer conference as the cultural framework for actions by student writers.

In 1989 we devised an electronic conference and repeated it for the next four years. The texts included in the conference focused on one topic—the original newspaper reports from the early days of the 1960 Sit-Ins. The teacher-directive, which served as the initial prompt introducing the Sit-Ins conference, asked the students to examine certain aspects of language use in the newspaper stories. Language use was the first "topic" that students encountered, though seldom the first they addressed. Instead, they were more likely to respond to issues keyed to both the text and the subtext issues in the newspaper stories. As reports of racial confrontation during the civil rights movement in the U.S.A., these stories presented historical and affective, even inflammatory, subtexts about, for example, race, confrontation, civil liberties, and violence. Each student's writing had its own hierarchy of issues, depending on how it addressed the teacher-directive, the general topic of the conference texts as a whole ("the Sit-Ins"), a particular newspaper story, ideas and issues in writings by other students, and the student's own comments in a previous writing. As soon as the conference discussion began, students became emotionally as well as intellectually involved. Although the students wrote about the verbs and modifiers used by the writers of the newspaper stories, they also analyzed the meaning or significance of those forms in terms of the news writers' stance and reflections of attitudes conveyed through those forms. In terms of modern philology, they engaged in "the study of the meaning of language forms as these depend on the linkage of signs to the context in which they occur" (Watkins 1989: 785).

When we introduced the Sit-Ins mainframe computer conferences to our students in 1989, we saw the conferences as a reserve shelf in a library that never closed, a chalkboard that was never erased, and a fieldwork record that included everybody's entries. As students began to write in the conferences, we recognized that they had engaged themselves in the difficult task of establishing norms for their temporary electronic community of writers as they chose ways to write about a socially sensitive subject. We chose to look at those aspects of students' uses of language that shift within specific contexts as the students wrote about practices and attitudes conveyed through language recorded before most of them were born.

As Stubbs (1996: 152–53) recommends in his principles for text analysis, our analysis of the corpus of the students' writing is comparative. We look at the full corpus, the individual in differently situated conferences, the individual topics, similar topics across all conferences, the first entries in all topics across a single conference, the narrative schema of all entries in a single topic, and all writings by single students across topics. We analyze specific features that sometimes characterize the corpus, sometimes a cohort of writers, sometimes a type or style of text, and most frequently, the individual writer. We archived and examined a corpus of language— collected from computer-naive users who wrote extemporaneously at the computer keyboard and interfaced with other texts—so that this corpus could be compared with features from other corpora of text, both within the electronic domain (such as electronic mail lists, netmail, and messages) and without.

From interactional sociolinguistics, we drew on methods for examining the multiparty and interactive nature of our text. From variationist sociolinguistics, we drew from methods of looking at the distribution of repetition and variation of features for individual and groups of writers. From the ethnographic and historical paradigms, we drew on the emphases of comparison across contexts, of natural description, of reconstruction of text, in order to examine communicative competence and performance. We began with the word, since that is where electronic conference discourse begins.

Electronic discourse is patterned, structured in multiple layers that can have, in the minimally hypertextual discourse of the electronic conference, multiple links. Throughout this study, we look at the ways the student writers legitimate their claims, opinions, ideas, insights, or responses by appeals either to the newspaper text, to some body of cultural knowledge about either the time of the Sit-Ins or the current scene that they take as given or shared, or to their own memories and life experiences. We note that their shorter writings generally fall into either a mode that is "guarded" or one that is "self-disclosing." If their writings are 150 words or longer, the individual writing will generally present both modes, or text types. We chose these modes or text types rather than Labov's terms, "casual" and "careful," because either (or both) of the text types can be presented in either casual or careful style. We show that the student writers' alternations between types, and the boundaries for those text types, are signaled by the shifts in type-token ratio that index density, repetition, and patterned variation at the lexical level.

We also analyze direct and indirect address because they are an important part of the interactive nature of this kind of writing. How students present themselves at the most general level through direct and indirect address involves a form of negotiation of identity as presented in, by, and through interactive electronic text. We look above the sentence level at successive levels of language and text, in order to delineate how the writers develop conventions for themselves and enculturate each other. The index for such conventions and enculturation is the use of repetition and emulation—repetition at the level of words or lexical collocation, and emulation for larger patterns, including syntactic features, narrative schemata, and communicative orientation. Both repetition and emulation are analyzed by tagging and sorting the features in our corpus. We hand tagged each feature or pattern described and used the computer to sort and generate a concordance of the tagged features.

Description of the corpus

Our corpus of electronic discourse consists of a set of three mainframe conferences from the first three consecutive semesters (1990–

1991) that we incorporated the conference into linguistics courses at both universities' campuses. The social situation varied each time. The first semester's conference (Stand Alone) had no interaction between campuses; the second conference (Exchange) was completed on each campus and then exchanged with the other, to elicit additional replies; the third (Transparent) linked students from both campuses simultaneously. The newspaper stories and our only directional prompt that appeared as the first item remained the same for each conference. Table 1.1 profiles the writers, entries, and words for the total corpus of 116,929 words. Based on 350 words of typescript for an 8 1/2 x 11 inch page, the corpus contains approximately 334 pages of conventional text. Table 1.1 gives a profile of the conferences.

Excluding dual writers, students who worked in dyads but used only one user name to write and send their comments, the proportion of female to male writers was almost 3 to 1, with females represented by 197 writers, with 89,474 words, and males represented by 71 writers, with 27,455 words. Females, however, wrote slightly more; although they represented 73.5 percent of the writers, they wrote 76.5 percent of the words. Additional correlations with gender are shown in Table 1.2, which organizes the corpus by lexical characteristics. "Token" represents the total of all words, "type" means the total of unique words, and "chunk" means the number of fifty-word segments.

Since the corpus is an artifact of written text, we approached it first at the lexical level, with two ways of organizing the text for analysis. We indexed the total corpus with a software program that enabled us to create a concordance of a word or grammatical tag

Table 1.1. Profile of the Electronic Conferences

	Entries	Writers	Words
Stand Alone UNCC fall 1990	163	30	20,174
Stand Alone UNCG fall 1990	79	23	12,049
Exchange UNCC spring 1991	230	74	25,048
Exchange UNCG spring 1991	281	73	31,785
Transparent fall 1991	226	68	27,873
Totals	979	268	116,929

Note: Writers from both campuses participated in the Exchange conferences.

Table 1.2. Lexical Characteristics

	Exchange UNCC	Exchange UNCG	Stand Alone UNCC	Stand Alone UNCG	Transparent	Totals
No. of Females	51	53	24	21	48	197
Tokens	16,999	31,785	16,207	11,130	20,783	48,120
Max	376	495	505	570	634	
Min	0	0	0	4	0	
Mean	108	113	117	150	127	
Types	5,667	12,063	6,532	5,836	9,838	22,206
Max	324	387	389	468	599	
Min	0	0	0	0	0	
Mean	36	43	47	79	60	
Chunks (est.)*	340.1	635.9	324.2	222.7	416.3	963.2
Max	7.5	9.9	10.1	11.4	12.7	
Min	0.0	0.0	0.0	0.1	0.0	
Mean	2.2	2.3	2.3	3.0	2.5	
No. of Males	23	20	6	2	20	71
Tokens	8,049	7,430	3,967	919	7,090	11,976
Max	450	347	446	346	303	
Min	0	0	8	8	0	
Mean	110	118	159	184	114	
Types	3281	2959	2775	622	2,224	5,621
Max	325	272	371	264	230	
Min	0	0	0	0	0	
Mean	45	47	111	124	36	
Chunks (est.)*	161.2	148.4	79.4	18.4	142.1	239.9
Max	9.0	6.9	8.9	6.9	6.1	
Min	0.0	0.0	0.2	0.2	0.0	
Mean	2.2	2.4	3.2	3.7	2.3	

*The number of estimated chunks = tokens/50

(done by hand for selected portions of the corpus). We also divided every writing into fifty-word segments of text in order to run type-token ratios on every writing presenting three or more fifty-word chunks.

Type-token ratio indicates the lexical diversity within a text by dividing the number of different words, or types, by the total number of words, or tokens, in segments of text. It has been used for studies of written and spoken language. For example, Carpenter (1990) based his study of depositions, oral testimony, and cross-examinations during a trial on earlier studies of written text as well as oral speech. He noted that for spoken text, the segments sub-jected to type-token ratio (TTR) analysis need to be at least twenty-five words in length: "Segments any shorter . . . are not fruitful for TTR analyses because the statistical probability is that native speakers of English do not utter statements of 10 to 15 words in length without repeating one of those words, and variations betweeen such smaller segments do not lend themselves to meaningful interpreta-tions" (Carpenter 1990, fn. 19: 16–17).

For our TTR analysis of electronic discourse, we used segments of fifty words. This segment length is practical and useful in analyz-ing electronic discourse because the analyst can study features used by individual writers as well as features used by groups of writers. This segment length is also roughly equivalent to a minute of unin-terrupted "speech" and half a screen of single-space writing in the "reply" function of VAXNotes, the mainframe software program used for our conferences. Electronic discourse—conferences, e-mail, dis-cussion lists, or forums—consists of the statements and perspectives of individual writers. Analyzing all conference or discussion list writing as a unified whole would be equivalent to analyzing a conversation, which by definition must include at least two speakers, as if only one speaker participated. For example, the sixty-eight writers in the Trans-parent conference discussion would be presented as a generalized, single individual. This approach eliminates the distinguishing feature of electronic discourse—the individual writer.

The fifty-word segment length allowed writers to present elabo-ration, setting a baseline for our comparisons and allowing us to examine variation and repetition across individuals with some de-gree of precision. TTR measures the variation for an individual speaker or writer rather than for a group, in that it indicates the individual's variation from his or her mean. A segment with a TTR higher than the mean for that writer's statements would indicate more diversity and less repetition. Changes of TTR within succes-sive segments of discourse signal that the level of lexical diversity has changed, suggesting some sort of shift in style.

Throughout our discussion, we call these segment "chunks," for the same reason as Barbara Johnstone in her *Stories, Community and Place*; we want "to avoid prejudging the issue of what these larger units are" (Johnstone 1990: 41). We found that these fifty-word chunks had a nice fit with the average length of segments of narrative when we reanalyzed the writings using a framework adapted from Labov (1972): orientation, narrative(s), and coda. Table 1.3 uses different type fonts and markings to show this fit.

Comparing features of electronic discourse has led us to hypothesize something about an otherwise unobservable pair of phenomena, which we call by the metaphoric term "chiming." In interactive electronic discourse, the writer is a reader, a writer, and a thinking communicator. Writers chime into text that they have read, calling on their repertoires of styles and competencies in both speaking and writing. As they write responses, they (probably unconsciously) present features into which their presumed readers may chime. In effect, they "charm" a reader into reading the whole of their text, using repetition to signal direct assent or alignment with a position—an opinion or a stance—and emulation to present more indirect agreement.

Using the concordance: An example

Interaction among a number of factors underlie shifts of style among segments of a text; TTR signaled that shifts had taken place, and the concordancer provided in the WordCruncher software program allowed us both to look in more detail at specific aspects that might underlie a particular shift and to examine larger patterns of usage for lexical or grammatical features. Our analysis of the use of the intensifier "a lot" can illustrate how we used the corpus. Both "a lot", written as two words, and "alot", written as one word, occur in our data. We consider the two spellings in free variation and thus as the same collocation. The choice of a particular intensifier, such as "a lot" will be maintained throughout entries by a specific person; its appearance is usually in segments that depart from the writer's mean TTR, in either direction, by one or more standard deviations. "A lot" occurs in three well-attested usages in our data: (1) as an intensifier, as in "a lot more carefully" (see Quirk, Greenbaum, Leech and Svartvik 1972: 295); (2) as a partitive, as in "a lot of hype" (ibid.); and (3) as a noun phrase, as in "gave them a lot" (ibid., cf. section #5.77).

Twenty of the sixty-eight writers in the Transparent Conference presented twenty-eight uses of *a lot/alot*, with females more frequent

Table 1.3. Narrachunks: The Overlap of Narrative and TTR Segments

This figure illustrates the correlation of onset/orientation, narrative and coda with TTR-segments

Transparent Conference, Entry 2.17

'Shandie' uses her first name in the title (coda) as part of the "Titling Game" that took place in Topic 2 of the Transparent Conference. Her orientation indirectly refutes Writing 212 with an empathetic reframing of the 1960s newspaper writer's position. Her frame, by setting up her location of self as being born after the 60s (Writing 209 had located self in that time period), mitigates her claims to 'given knowledge' about that time period while drawing on her own personal experience, and allows her to project and hedge how she might or might not have acted at that time (Writings 213 and 216 had engaged in projection). She evaluates and sets up a new orientation, reflecting on the newspaper article, to frame her final segment. This segment looks at the wording in the article itself, beginning with "orderly" (a word from the newspaper story studied in Writing 202) ending with an evaluation of the style as being in conflict with the time period of the 60s: her final evaluation echoes the time set forth in the initial orientation, and she writes the Title as her Coda to the whole writing.

Coding:
　　　　// marks end of line　　　　* marks TTR-chunk separation　　　# marks beginning, new sentence

Narrative Schema:

Coda 3: Title for whole writing [last thing written]
Orientation to first and all successive narratives until the SHIFT
Narrative 1
Narrative 2
Coda 1, evaluation from Narratives 1 and 2 / Orientation to third narrative
TTR SHIFT: FROM MEDIUM TO HIGHEST TTR
Narrative 3　　　　Highest TTR
TTR SHIFT: FROM HIGHEST TO LOWEST TTR
Coda 2: Evaluation of Narrative 3, lowest TTR

Coda-3	1	-< shandie's thoughts >-
Orientation	2	*i thought that the article was sympathetic for the time in which it was //
	3	written. #i don't think that they gave enough information about the //
	4	facts as they were but then again,i don't think it would be possible //
	5	seeing as how everyone views things differently
		#the issues of civil //
Narr-1	6	*rights are interesting to me yet i really don't understand why the //
	7	black population was treated this way to begin with. #i know this is //
	8	probably because i did not grow up in this span of time and i have //
	9	always gone to desegregated schools
		#it makes me feel strange to think//
Narr-2	10	*about not having gone to school with all different races.# i think it //
	11	has helped me get a better outlook on different cultures and to become //
	12	a more well-rounded person. #i would like to think that i would not //
(Eval)	13	have treated the afro-americans this way if i had been alive back then //
Coda-1	14	*but i cannot honestly say that because i don't know what it was like//
Orientation	15	#the article itself surprises me by being sympathetic at a time when no //
	16	one of the white population wanted to have anything to do with civil //
HI TTR	17	rights. #it really surprised me to read the word "orderly" describing //
Narr3	18	*the blacks [sic] students as they were leaving the store. # the wording used //
	19	makes the white people look worse mannered than the black students. # i //
LO TTR	20	think the writer of this article deserves great credit for his/her //
	21	choice of words. #the style chosen is in direct conflict with the actual //
Coda-2		
	22	*tumultuous times of the 60's civil rights movement.//

in terms of total tokens, but males more frequent relative to size of cohort (nine of twenty males; eleven of forty-eight females). Table 1.4 lists writers by gender and a number assigned to mask student identity; the number following the colon is the number of times that student used *a lot* in a particular way.

Notice that only five of these uses are "true" intensives; the only writers who use the nominalized formation are also those who write more than 150 words. If a writer uses *a lot* more than once, the writer (as with F2, F6, M6, F8) will tend to continue using it in the same way. In other words, the partitive is more common than either the intensifier or the nominalization from the partitive, but the use of any of these is driven by idiolectal preference.

One of the most interesting aspects of our study has been the notion of idiolect and the individual's discourse signature in electronic discourse. Writing in the electronic universe, people adapt conventions of oral and written discourse to their own, individual communicative ends, as when they draw on modality or develop interactive strategies keyed to the formulaic properties of rhetorical questions or the dramatic potential of "asides." Electronic discourse presents us with texts in contact, and through those texts, their writers. We have sought evidence for change, some trace of being and human interaction in a domain where footprints are not in moon dust but in ether.

Table 1.4. Use of *a lot* by type and gender

	Type 1 *Intensive*	Type 2 *Partitive*	Type 3 *Nominal*
TTR-writings (150+ words)	F1: 1	F2: 4	F2: 1
		M1: 1	M2: 2
		M3: 1	M4: 1
		F3: 1	F4: 1
non-TTR writings			
(fewer than 150 words)	F5: 1	F6: 2	M9: 1
	M5: 1	M6: 2	F9: 1
	F7: 1	F8: 2	F10: 1
	M7: 1	M8: 1	F11: 1

2:// Context and contact in electronic discourse

In 1989, looking for a way to help students to see a convergence between theory and practice in linguistic analysis, we drew on our own experience with on-line communications to create a mainframe computer conference on the 1960s Sit-Ins as a fieldwork simulation for them. We teach at two campuses in a state university system—the University of North Carolina at Charlotte and the University of North Carolina at Greensboro. The campuses, each with its own distinctive character, are ninety miles apart. We wanted students to look at ways usage might index historical or cultural events, so that their study of language usage during a particular historical period might go beyond simplistic or trivial shibboleths. We thought that examining language use in an earlier period of time could focus students on the kinds of attitudes about language that they as speakers and writers had unknowingly formed about language variety. Most of all, we wanted students to marvel at the complexities, the rich interrelationships among the different systems of language and of the levels of language usage, and to see that marvel from the inside, as active, questioning learners.

A conference might give our students a miniature fieldwork experience that had a beginning, an end, and a point. We expected the conference to provide a setting in which shy students with southern politeness conventions in large classes could exchange ideas and opinions on hot issues of race, power, and gender. The framework had to have some boundaries, some scaffolding: if too difficult to access or operate, the students' frustration would halt their participation. If marked overtly for any particular interpretation, their suspicion would impede expression. If unrelated to class goals and anticipated course content, their enthusiasm would diminish.

We used the VAXNotes mainframe software program to create a conference of newspaper texts on the emergence of the Sit-Ins of the sixties, and added a prompt that asked students to focus some attention on language usage in those texts. 1990 was the thirtieth anniversary of the Sit-Ins, which started at a Greensboro lunch counter, spread swiftly to Charlotte, and then swept across the south as a part of the emerging civil rights movement in the U.S.A. We scanned two weeks of local news stories in the chronological order that they "broke" and were covered by the *Greensboro Record*, the *Greensboro Daily News*, the *Charlotte News*, and the *Charlotte Observer*. At the time of the Sit-Ins, both Charlotte and Greensboro had morning and evening newspapers. The conference prompt was:

> The ARTICLE conference is a collection of newspaper articles taken from the beginning of the period of the sit-ins. Please read and respond to a minimum of four notes. Pay particular attention to the shades of meaning in verbs, modifiers, titles and honorifics.

Writers in our conferences were not anonymous writers. They frequently signed their personal names, though this was not required. The software program displayed their personal userids on each entry, instead of disguised names or nicknames. We chose never to write in the conferences, lest we unwittingly seem to privilege, disparage, or question the validity of any individual entry. We felt that our initial prompt would be enough interference with whatever kind of interaction and conference culture might evolve. We discussed with them our role as participant-observers, and examined with them a variety of issues about anonymity, disclosure, and writing in a public arena that might be expected to surface even within a private conference.

The conferences were closed to people outside the classes unless students invited or permitted others to read or view the writing. The students knew that we would occasionally log on and visit their conferences, and that we as well as they would read what they wrote. They knew they were operating in a public mode because the conference, like any conferencing system, presented every message written by any participant. We announced that students could print their conference contributions at any time, and that we would print out the full conference at term's end so that they could photocopy both their contributions and the writings of their peers. In our brief, in-class training sessions, we pointed out how the computer program logged their userids, the time and date, and the number of lines written each time they signed on. As warm-ups for the conferences, we set up a sequence of real-world assignments, which allowed students first to test their own comfort with participant-observer situations; next, to draw from those experiences for our class-conducted discussions on fieldwork ethics; and finally to move into discussions of handling sensitive issues. We used exercises such as identifying gender cues in tag questions collected from conversations and conducting brief surveys of usage ("quarter to, quarter of, or quarter 'til five") with random campus groups.

Students "knew" that the conference was theirs, that we would not edit what they wrote, that we would "visit" only in order to learn from the conference comments, that we would mediate only if requested (we never were), and that we would not grade their electronic conference writing for content, issues, opinions, or mechanics. Instead, the evaluative measure applied was "Did you do the work during the time officially announced for the conferences? Did you contribute your ideas, views, and insights to the discussions in the conferences?" The conference program recorded the date and time of the conference contributions for both us and the students. Students knew from the outset of the course that one class requirement was participation in the conference, and they generally considered the writing in it to be analogous to that in a journal or log.

During the period a conference was running, we never discussed any of its content or issues in class meetings, nor were we ever asked to do so. The only questions we received were concerned with logistics: for example, the sequence for log-ins, problems with commands in the conferencing software, or the speed of the mainframe on a given day. At the close of the conferences, the students wrote and handed in papers discussing their experience in the new medium, and their reflections on how they had learned what they had learned. Students could draw from their own writing and from the writing by anyone in the conference for their discussions. We keyed grading to a holistic rubric developed in collaboration between students and instructors with an instructor-imposed limit on the maximum number of pages to be submitted. Before archiving the conferences and analyzing features of electronic discourse, we discussed research on electronic discourse with the students, assuring them of both privacy and anonymity, with pseudonyms to be used in referring to particular entries and written statements of permission to quote material with attribution.

Repetition in electronic conference discourse

When readers move from examining the word- and phrase-level repetition characteristic of spoken discourse to the longer stretches of repetition in the uninterrupted discourse presented by written text, they bump up against several problems, usually centered on how they are to say what the text "means." For example, written texts often present the suggestion of phonological and nonverbal cues, but the presentation is likely to be ambiguous and the author can seldom be contacted for fuller explanation. Electronic conference discourse presents the problems of any set of written texts, and adds a few wrinkles of its own. For one thing, is the student's writing in the conferences characteristic of the writer? For the analysis of speech, the researcher often tries to come as close as possible to eliciting "natural language"—that is, unprompted, unselfconscious, uninterrupted, untainted (by the elicitor) language which can be seen as characteristic of the speaker's habits and the speaker's largely unconscious conventions of or preferences for expression (Labov 1972:208–9). While we certainly cannot claim that the electronic conference discourse we analyze in this study is "natural written language," and we don't know what that would be, we do claim that the corpus as a whole comes fairly close to being characteristic of the writers' habits and preferences in certain kinds of writing, and may even suggest habits and preferences in oral discourse.

One prominent feature of our corpus was repetition. Students repeated key words, phrases, grammatical structures, and discourse strategies from the articles they read, from other students' writing, or from their own experience as they wrote their entries for the conferences. As in a conversation they used repetition as one means of sustaining the discussion of particular ideas, arguments, opinions, and feelings related to materials they read. As we discuss in detail in a later chapter, students repeated names, synonyms for verbs, and alliterative phrases in their titles as part of a word play game that they sustained throughout a topic or throughout the entire conference. As Tannen notes, "repetition is at the heart of language: in Hymes's terms, language structure, in Bolinger's, language production, in Becker's, all languaging" (1989:46).

There is a dynamic relationship between reported events and students' interpretations of the language used to report those events. Repetition provided a framework into which the students placed new information, a scaffold with which students could approach even the most controversial subjects. Repetition at word or phrase level could begin with the first posting; patterns of emulation began to develop after there was some sort of critical mass, which seems to have been no sooner than the third posting and no later than the fifth. We tested this claim by looking at patterns established by all first postings in each conference topic, at patterns throughout all entries in a single conference topic, and at patterns in all entries by a single writer, posted to any topic during the duration of the conference.

On the macrolevel, a student's narrative could repeat another writing's sequence of rhetorical strategies, with each strategy usually constituting a different frame in the narrative. At this level of text, the most frequent pattern was the claim-warrant pattern. A student writer presented an assertion about the text(s) read, and this assertion, a frame in itself, included other frames, either a shift to different topics or to the use of different rhetorical strategies, which were equivalent to different speech acts in conversation. Any of these could be repeated, quoted, cited, or emulated.

In the example below, from his first two writings, Brandon used assertion to put forward a claim of evaluation, which gave him the choice to justify his claim by presenting either personal experience, "known" facts about the events, or personal interpretation of the language in the text. Brandon repeated key phrases (and a problem with subject-verb agreement) from his own earlier posting in the same topic. The numbering of each student reply is furnished by VAXNotes: 2.21 is the 21st reply appended to topic 2, and 4.24 is the 24th reply under topic 4:

2.21 This particular report on the sit-ins is one that contained a general use of language in order to maintain an objective perspective. The events were relayed to the audience in a very nonchalant manner which seemed to disguise the actual ugliness of the situation. The use of words in the article were evidently thought out and the phrases were well planned so the author would suffer no repercussions. . . .

4.24 Here again, I noticed a nonchalant use of language. The emotions involved in these racial incidents were basically told from the white perspective. The only things that the African-American students were asked were how they were going about protesting without violence and what their next move would be. I personally feel that this particular news report was biased. . . .

Repetition above the lexical level is perhaps better seen as emulation, since the repetition is of pattern or strategy, rather than of lexical or phrasal elements. Emulation, as a kind of imitation, involves the selection and appropriation of larger patterns. Like an oral poet, selecting from a repertoire of patterns, figures, tropes, and other elements in order to create or perform an epic tale, the students in the electronic conferences drew upon their own repertoires of experience with oral and written discourse to respond both to the texts created in the 1960s and to texts newly created by other students in the conferences They repeated words and phrases from these texts, often extending morphological formations. They also appropriated and adapted larger patterns, such as the strategy of using rhetorical questions, which they must have seen as potentially useful for their own purposes in conveying their meaning.

In general, the first three student responses appended to the newspaper stories, in any of the conference topics, gave permission to successive writers to emulate larger patterns in some or all of the following ways, by ways they presented:

(a) presence or absence of response to the teacher-prompt for the conference, which had asked that attention be paid to particular features of language usage;

(b) presence/absence of self-disclosure of personal values or opinions in response to the newspaper text;

(c) presence/absence of disclosure of personal knowledge of the time or events in the newspaper text;
(d) presence/absence of claim-warrant discourse (the most frequent rhetorical strategy invoked) keyed to presumably shared knowledge about the time or events in the newspaper text;
(e) presence/absence of embedded narratives of personal experience or emotive reaction to the newspaper text's style, format, details, events as narrated or described, etc.

Emulation can be viewed as a situation-cued process of developing standards in a community. In her study of the process of Anglicization of written Scottish English, Devitt (1989) reminds us that linguistic standardization is a historical process; Ferguson (1994: 21) reminds us that a genre, "literary or nonliterary, emerges in a specific sociohistorical context." The writing in the electronic conferences had context and history, even if these were brief. The students, with community conferred upon them, developed conventions, which acted as standards, and exchanged information during that interaction. The students used repetition and emulation as basic processes in creating and maintaining their discourse. Despite the short period of time during which the conferences took place, we could identify some features of language contact and change, signaled primarily by repetition and emulation. Despite its ephemerality, some notion of discourse community was apparently at work.

In one sense, an entire conference is a discourse that consists of individual students' comments about whatever topic is discussed. It is easy to lose sight of the individual through the creation of a textual artifact that, when completed, is not the writing of any single individual or a focused collaboration of multiple individuals with the goal of creating a single voice. One key to understanding the nature of the text resides in the analysis of the individual's usage of word- and phrase-level repetition and the emulation of discourse strategies.

The messages in electronic conference discourse are electronic texts that present a sense of immediacy described as characteristic of spoken discourse. They read like individual turns although they are actually written messages stored in an electronic mail box or bin. The bin in VAXNotes is the topic with all the students' replies dated, identified by userid, and filed with a subnumber. There is no real turn taking in electronic conference discourse. Instead, there is an asynchronous exchange of messages about a particular topic. It is through that exchange that we can say contact occurs in electronic conference discourse: the contact is not with the other students but with the texts that the students have left behind.

In *A Chorus Line*, each person steps forward and tells an individual story. The collection and juxtaposition of individual perspectives and stories create the play. In electronic conference discourse, each student steps forward to present a perspective, an idea, an argument, or a personal experience related to the prompt or to another student's perspective or idea. The collection and juxtaposition of their comments creates the complete conference text. We must look to individual repetition and emulation in order to understand the separate parts and the combined nature of that text.

Our analyses of conference samples identified patterns keyed to the idiolect of individual writers; that is, their individual and habitual shifts between what Biber called "informational" and "involved" dimensions of text. Biber's study is concerned with the relationship between speech and writing; our study looks at writing, which reads in part as if the writers were speaking—which may account for the many informal on-line discussions in the late 1980s of why computer-mediated communication might be more like speech than writing: see, for example, the review of studies of electronic communication in Wilkins (1991).

An emergent register

The corpus of electronic conference discourse was doubly situated, with both a physical and a social setting. Examining issues of social variables, such as setting and the larger issue of conventionalization or standardization, requires looking at notions of community, regardless of how short a time that community is operable, and must at some point deal with issues of register and genre to see which best accounts for features of text or community organization. Although we examine idiolectal maintenance and style shift in electronic conference discourse, we suspect that this type of electronic conference discourse is not, in itself, a genre, though it and the very different form of electronic communication, messaging, may come to be seen as a register. The channel or medium through which electronic conference discourse is distributed is relatively recent and the time for its use by the students, and their time to form some sort of short-lived community, was relatively brief.

The distinctions made by Ferguson (1994) are helpful here: the *register* marks a particular communication situation as different from other situations; the *genre* is a recurrent message type within a community. There are two additional reasons for us to be cautious here. First, as written text, conference discourse—perhaps like any "unplanned," extemporaneous composing—often includes those features more generally associated with speech acts (d'Andrade and Wish 1990) or with what Biber (1988, 1994) calls an "involved" dimension, in order to characterize spoken or written texts where the producer's concern is to effect or maintain an involvement with the recipient. Second, conference discourse closely resembles some of those factored by Biber from already well-recognized genres. If we were to assign conference discourse to a genre of written text, it would be to the genre of public correspondence intended for an audience beyond the intimate. The student writings in the conference corpus could be seen as generically marked or typified for this rather broad genre if we consider the rhetorical situation of being in a class as the equivalent of work leading to professional acceptance, with responding to a task as equivalent to expecting a certain level of professionally cued metalanguage.

Since Keith Basso's taxonomy of letters in his study of the ethnography of writing (Basso 1974), contemporary scholars have been looking at audience-cued distinctions such as *public* and *private* as they apply to the classification of letters. Devitt's study of the process of standardization in written Scottish English drew on a distinction between official and personal correspondence, which was "based on the apparent relationship between writer and reader as expressed in the address or closing" (Devitt 1989:107). Biber's 1988 study of spoken and written texts included professional, editorial, and personal letters, though the dimensions he established were focused on the professional and personal (see his situational framework for the analysis of register; Biber 1994: 40–41). There are two features, however, which differentiate conference writing from professional, editorial, or official letters: they are the hallmarks of such letters, their greeting or salutation and their complimentary close. While some sort of acts of greeting and closing are part of the interchange in real-time electronic messaging (Murray 1989,1991), their order is reversed in asynchronous electronic discourse, since the title, which is often software-indexed and which serves as a sort of greeting in a directory or listing of writings, is actually the last thing composed.

While writers to bulletin boards or mail-lists occasionally present an additional greeting in the body of their message, particularly if they are new members, they more frequently quote or refer to a previous posting as a replacement for the salutation. And while some writers will employ a short closing, such as "Cheers" or "Peace," participants on bulletin boards or electronic mailing lists sometimes substitute a signature, which often includes, in addition to electronic and nonelectronic addresses, a quotation or motto. Neither of these are present in our corpus of electronic conference discourse. We think it is because the conference, which serves a different purpose, is seen as a closed grouping within which such formalities are unnecessary.

When we separated out the closing statements, considering them to be whatever preceded the final mark of punctuation, we noticed that once again, emulation was at work. Statements such as "More later" or "I'll get back to you" made by some writers in their individual first entries were gone by their second entries, replaced by what they evidently saw as the more conventional, a summary of whatever they had just written. This suggests that standardization— for that is the impact of emulation—was taking place at the outermost frame or at the level of discourse strategy.

The students in contact with each others' texts, whether from a single class on a single campus, in exchange with another campus, or joined at the mainframe in the transparent conference, emulated each others' larger patterns of discourse, such as titling, the use of direct and indirect address, or the strategy of posing rhetorical questions. Their repetition and emulation occurred at the level of word, phrase, clause, sentence pattern, and discourse strategy. Their preferences for *whether* they wanted to manifest style- or register-shifting may have been evoked by their desire to align themselves with or disaffiliate from the responses in writing of other student writers, but their preferred idiolectal patterns for *how* they did this remained relatively stable for each student. It may be that their efforts to emulate each other's rhetorical or discourse strategies were an adjustment to the medium, which was both physical and cultural. In the absence of face-to-face conversational cuing and turn taking, they modified and adapted conversational strategies to their own ends, combining their idiolectal preferences with emulation of syntactic and discourse patterns presented by other writers.

Electronic conferences as "Town meetings"

One metaphor that students used in later discussions of their computer conference as a fieldwork experience was that of a simulated city, with the topics as the different subdivisions and the individual userid as a house address. All sorts of spaces were brought into play since an electronic house has many rooms: memory, private life, personal views, story-telling habits, presuppositions, previous experience with written and oral text. In *Invisible Rendezvous*, Rob Wittig discusses how the denizens and projects of in.s.omnia, the Seattle-based electronic bulletin board, expanded the metaphor of "the invisible city of the ignored, the imperceptible, and the impossible" (Wittig 1994: 43ff.). Because of the elastic nature of boundaries in electronic space—like the MOOs of the 90s, the Seattle bulletin board system could add a "room," and the Sit-Ins conferences could add a new topic section—the new voyagers in the electronic universe often spent some time discussing metaphors such as "mapping" or "voyaging" or "cities" as one way of getting their bearings, of locating themselves in this new experience where a screen of text is not only the way people communicate their existence to each other, it is the existence. The ship and the voyager, the city and its inhabitant are the same thing: a text. As an educational setting, the conference provided convenience: travel was involved, but the students did not have to move off campus. Familiarity was reinvoked by our putting them back into worlds of discourse they already knew, such as letters, diaries, journals, and essays piled on top of a lifetime's history of conversation.

With the Sit-Ins conferences, we had called a town meeting. In the discussions, both vociferous and shy students had a floor, a turn, and a frame. We created a locus, provided an initial topos, and affected notions of time and space by rearranging notions of audience for three different years of conferences. In this study, we have called the 1990 conference the Stand Alone: each instructor mounted the conference on each campus separately, and students had classroom opportunity for face-to-face clarification or further discussion. The 1991 conference was the Exchange: after students on each campus participated in the conference mounted on that campus, the instructors exchanged the conference files and students wrote replies to those writers from the other campus. The 1991–92 conferences were Transparent: linked by a local mainframe network (DECNET), the conference "appeared" on each campus whenever accessed by students at either place, so that both campuses entered their writings simultaneously. As the participants' sense of audience varied, so did the conventions they used, as they accommodated to each other, emulating each other in different ways, just as speakers of different languages in contact may create a pidgin, or speakers of different dialects in contact may temporarily shift register or other features.

The content of each of the conferences was the same: an initial prompt of directions from us as instructors, and the series of newspaper stories about the Sit-Ins. By asking students to consider features of metadiscourse—language about language, or what Lucy (1993b) and others call reflexive language—we made them participant-observers in a world that had shaped their own. They traveled through electronic time and space to arrive at the time of the beginning of the civil rights sit-ins. They participated in those events as readers of the events as they occurred. They observed the events as visitors or outsiders from another time and space, and their initial writings were often from this perspective. As they began to write about the events described and the language used to convey the information about those events, they moved from observation into participation. They operated at two levels of time as they responded to what other students wrote and to the writers of articles about the original events as they occurred.

Most students moved beyond a formal or informal content analysis of an article: they used self-disclosure; they signaled affect; they engaged in direct and indirect reply to each other, drawing on lexico-grammatical, rhetorical, and discourse strategies to signal their awareness of other people in the conferences. Each person writing in the conference was writing monologue, for there could be no interruptions, no turn taking, no bids for the floor. But when reading, when planning writing, and when titling a writing and saving it to the conference, each participant engaged in dialogue, and it is that dialogue that is reflected in their increasingly complex acts of indirect response.

Did all the students so engage? Most of them, most of the time. Students who read and responded only to the newspaper prompts were few indeed. Curiosity to overhear or to look in on a "conversation" is a compelling force. Even students who chose to respond only to the newspaper prompts may have been engaged in some way. We simply do not have evidence in terms of direct address to a peer or of indirect address, the repetition or allo-repetition of a word, phrase, syntactic pattern, or rhetorical strategy, that documents those student's reference to another student's writing. For whatever reason, they chose to stay on the margins of a developing conversation. Multiparty conversation (Goodwin and Duranti 1992, Grimshaw 1990) presents a range or continuum for how much the participants talk. The same is true in electronic discourse, although you see, not hear, in different ways. The students were in contact with each other through language and the creation of text; the texts to and from each other were the students' primary reward. They accommodated each other as they accomodated to each other.

Trudgill (1986) provides an excellent discussion of contact and accommodation; Milroy (1990) offers an overview of social networks as they are keyed to speech. Here, we work more humbly, interested in shifts and networks in patterns of discourse beyond the phonological level, more in the tradition of looking at written language recently reestablished as a province for linguists by Tannen (1987, 1989) and Chafe (1986), or of looking at story-telling as a framework for identity as presented by Johnstone (1990, 1996). Like Tannen and Johnstone, we have drawn on repetition as the signpost to interpretation of context, contact, and community formation.

Changing contexts within a conference

Even when the social context for the conference shifted, by presenting students in the Transparent conference with an expanded audience of strangers from a different campus, students used the same devices. In the Exchange conferences, students followed the same norms. The first student from the other campus gave permission by example for direct/indirect address; successive writers followed his lead for at least five replies before departing from the pattern, whatever it was. Changing the pattern was like moving to another "room" or visiting another "house" in the neighborhood in order to join a different conversation or to create a new one. In the Transparent conference, students employed direct address primarily to students from their own campus, though in each topic one hardy writer usually moved into clearly marked direct address to a writing (never a writer) from the other campus. Successive writers from that campus joined in to the writing from their classmate for about five writings—that is, about five entries written in a topic in the conference.

It usually took about five writings, in which old topoi were indexed and new ones introduced, before any break with either the first topos or the successively linked ones could be made. Perhaps this is a signal of an electronic discourse boundary across all levels of discourse (from macrofeature to morpheme). Complaints about the computer were seldom echoed, and flaming of any kind was discouraged either by "silence" or by the addressee's shift into formal, even frozen (Joos 1967), style and an admonitory tone signaled by passive voice, a shift from "I" to "we, you, they, one," and repetition of part of the instructors' prompt. Disagreement abounded, but it was civil; reactions were deep, and they were expressed as personal opinion and experience whose truth value usually cannot be contested openly without bringing shame to the writer. On the average, someone would summarize all of the responses, both directly and indirectly, after eight to ten replies to any given topic had been written, and the discussion would resume.

Some purposes behind repetition in electronic discourse

The repetitive, rambling, discursive, recursive features of electronic conference writing may actually, then, serve the purpose of creating community among its writers, even though that community is short-lived. We suggest that electronic conference writing is a new register in written electronic discourse, more complex than one would at first assume, and a worthy object of close and detailed scrutiny

if we are to understand the cognitive and social interplay of dis·
course features. Conference register, at least in the argumentative
mode that the Sit-Ins conferences evoke, has specific norms and
turns, progressive acculturation and enculturation. As Brent wrote
privately to us, using the impersonal *it*, which staged most expres-
sions of personal surprise throughout the conference: "it was strange.
I found myself visiting the sixties with the mindset of the eighties,
using the technology of the nineties."

When we move beyond the linear organization of a text, to look
at how different parts may connect with each other in meaningful
ways, we, like Brown and Yule (1983), see Grimes's (1975) metaphor of "staging" as useful. This metaphor allows researchers to
look at how people recall or interpret stretches of text. Whatever
comes first, colors everything that follows, whether it is the title of
a story, the headline of a newspaper report, or the initial words in
the first clause of a speech: "That is, we assume that every sentence
forms part of a developing, cumulative instruction which tells us
how to construct a coherent representation" (Grimes 1975: 134).

Student writers in the Sit-Ins conferences apparently self-moni-
tored their extemporaneous keyboard composing to some extent,
writing around and into what they wanted to say, halting and start-
ing over, initiating new themes on occasion, thematizing content-
bearing words in order to stage what they finally wanted to communicate. The metaphor of staging can then include the way a writer
"stages" discourse by means of a variety of rhetorical devices including repetition. Looking at staging, thematization, and topicali-
zation is one way to understand the ways people interpret and recall
text. The student writers in our conference, who could see on their
screens only seven lines of text at any moment, suggest by their
multilayered written repetition the ways they had for focusing on
theme, on staging, and on topics that engaged them as readers and
thinkers.

They used repetition for multiple purposes, to signal a variety of
speech acts and to show agreement or disagreement, alignment or
disaffiliation, with the writing-cum-thinking of the other writers in
the conference; they worked in their repetition at several levels. And
each student had individual patterns, which we will discuss in terms
of "idiolect." Each student's preferred patterns of emphasis or style
shifting held constant for that student across topic. In responding to

the writings of others, students most frequently "chimed in" to whatever signaled affect. Affect, most often made prominent by clause- or sentence-initial position, served as an invitation, whether at the lexical level with content-bearing words and their formal extensions (*race . . . racial . . . racism*), at clause- and sentence-level with syntactic patterns ("It is important to . . ." "I feel sorry that . . ."), or at levels such as direct address.

In creating their own writings, students presented a continuum of words, phrases, clauses, and rhetorical strategies that could display affect and allow or invite others to chime in. For example, the pattern of Minda's closing in her posting to topic 4 was echoed by other writers intermittently through the next ten postings, as shown by Sally's closing, which even emulated Minda's all-caps writing:

4.27   ANY INDIVIDUAL INVOLVED IN THE KKK IS AN IDIOT. I COMPLETELY DISAGREE WITH THE CONCEPT OF WHITE SUPREMACY. GIVE ME A BREAK.

4.28   JUST LET EVERYONE BE AND DO WHATEVER THEY HELL THEY WANT. THERE IS TOO MANY PROBLEMS IN THIS WORLD AS IT IS. JUST GIVE IT A REST.

The conference writings presented a variety of patterns. Hymes has noted for oral interaction that "there is a further level, a level of interaction and speech events, a level at which the distribution of speech acts, their weighting and hierarchy, their relations to each other, are patterned" (Hymes 1990). We saw this level not only in the body of the writings, but also in the titles the students devised. These titles were important staging devices; frequently exhibiting repetition themselves, they helped the reader form a schema for interpretation by presenting a variety of cues. As we discuss later, titles could function to furnish the reader with the setting and scene into which reader/writer could enter as co-participants.

The multilayered use of repetition, what Tannen calls "allo-repetition," and of emulation, which we call "chiming," was characteristic of the writings throughout the conference. It was, we think, the primary means of signaling communicative intent to other participants, and thus became the means for the ephemeral social organization and enculturation during the conference.

3:// Entering the conferences: Challenges of time and space

Electronic writing: The "early" period

Students writing in our on-line mainframe conferences most often composed at the keyboard. At first glance, their writing, like many first drafts, might seem repetitive, recursive, discursive, even rambling, plagued by typographical errors and grammatical glitches. It was all of these, and it was more, we think. It was, like conversation, purposeful in what seemed to be acts of chaos, fractalized in this new medium, which promoted and preserved conversation like features for written text. It was capable of subtle variation in cohesion and coherence: created at the keyboard, read on the screen, transmitted in the air, able to be printed, and replete with variation among the larger patternings for groups as well as in the individual idiolects of the conference.

What if this corpus included the only texts we had from the beginnings of an early period of writing? Suppose, for example, that these were the texts redeemed from a Hittite library or from Egyptian hieroglyphic seals, from inscriptions in Attic Greek or palimpsests in Anglo-Saxon? We would be eager to explore the full dimensions of the writing context, interested in inferring the literacy conditions of the participants, intrigued by the gradual evolvement of a community of writers. And that corpus is what we have collected from novices in a virtual scriptorium. As novices, they were new to keyboarding and often nervous about computer technology, new to the conferencing software program and to the primary source material for the conferences themselves. Our corpus of computer-conference texts was written over three semesters, from 1990 to 1991, by students on two university campuses. The writers were unfamiliar with mainframes and largely unaware that they were in a situation that linguists might call "contact." We wanted text from the beginning of a new medium for language use by everyday people in everyday settings, what might be an early period in computer conference writing. That is, instead of text interchanged among expert or professional mainframe users, these writings were exchanged among students working with an application in a virtual classroom. The corpus collected over this period consists of the conference writings by 175 students in seven sections of six courses. Since the students wrote an average of fifty-plus lines for their average of four entries, the corpus is approximately 8,750 text lines (exclusive of software mastheads) on an 80-space monitor screen, or between 335 and 350 pages of conventional running text.

We expected that electronic conference writing, like other language events, would present features of variation and change. We looked at the ways students used language over the course of each full conference during a particular semester, over the course of a single topic within a conference, and over the three years during which we repeated the conferences, varying the degree of interaction between the two college campuses whose students participated in the conferences. We learned to study the recursiveness and the ramblings within the texts, finding in those features the key to how students used language to sustain ephemeral community , both within particular topics throughout a conference, and across campus borders, whether real or projected.

The subject of the conferences: What students brought as "given"

In the conferences, students found the familiar genre of news reports. The general topic of the Sit-Ins had important implications for society and schooling, although the reported events had taken place decades earlier. In this way, students traveled through *virtual time* to an earlier era, visiting a time of social unrest and civil rights demonstrations. They added to their experience the perspectives of writers who observed the events. Transporting themselves back into their own present, they reacted to the events and wrote about the way the newswriters had reported those events.

The year 1990 was the thirtieth anniversary of the civil rights Sit-Ins, which had begun in Greensboro, North Carolina, and had quickly spread to Charlotte, to other communities in the state, and across the southern part of the U.S.A. Locally, the University of North Carolina at Greensboro featured the anniversary as part of its campuswide university forum; regionally and nationally, newspapers and magazines ran retrospective news stories and features on the event. The majority of our students were not yet born when the sit-ins started, though they had lived with and through many of the events the civil rights movement sparked during the decade of the sixties. We realized that they had some general information about the civil rights movement, but little else surfaced in the informal interviews and class discussions we conducted the semester before the actual anniversary and implementation of the conference. They had some shared or given notions about the history of the period, largely culled from television documentaries and movies, from references in MTV videos, and occasionally, from junior- and senior-high school assignments during February, to commemorate black history month.

The predominant influences on their construct of the sixties, as cited by students in 1990s conversations, discussions, and postconferencing analyses, seem to have been the film *The Big Chill*, and also films and documentaries relating to black history such as *Eyes on the Prize* (documentary), the filmed drama of *Raisin in the Sun*, or the television series of *Roots*. Some students remembered clips of Martin Luther King rebroadcast on local news programs or excerpted from video-disk encyclopedias such as the *Video Encyclopedia of the Twentieth Century*. The expanded role for black comedians from 1985 to 1990, particularly Eddie Murphy, and for black film directors, particularly Spike Lee, was also presented in the students' discussion of MTV videos and montages as being a source for their shared or given knowledge. They brought varying degrees of sophistication to their construct of news media as well: students, most just turning twenty, assumed without question that articles on the front page were unbiased and had some difficulty distinguishing between features and news articles, particularly if the article had a by-line.

By 1991 most students had seen the film *Mississippi Burning*, and were beginning to read advance publicity for Spike Lee's *Malcolm X*. We must stress that we were not seeking to learn what students might have learned at one time, or only what they could remember unprompted, but instead what they, in a multiracial classroom thirty years after the events, were willing to share in a networked group discussion. Theirs was a fairly vague knowledge base if the students were under the age of thirty; older students who had lived through the time period had keen memories and few reservations about sharing them.

During the three years of our corpus collection, we also observed changes in the students' familiarity with technology. The students in the 1989 to 1990 classes had no familiarity with mainframes and little conscious experience with microcomputers. Our students, most of them in the humanities, had either missed the installation of computer labs in their high schools, or their teachers had not yet integrated microcomputers into their classes. A university junior in 1989 to 1990 would probably have been a junior in high school in 1985 to 1986 and, outside of work experience with cash registers or inventory data bases, usually had had little precollege experience with computers of any kind as a way to create or share text with others. By 1992 to 1993, however, as many as eighty percent of the students in some classes reported using computers at work; sixty percent regularly used the university's microcomputer labs for writing and printing papers; more than half reported high school experience with keyboard composition; and forty percent either had brought a computer or a word processor to college, or had lined up a roommate who had one.

Setting and participants: A closer look

We had originally designed the conference so that all the students could become aware of usage conventions within their historical context, using primary source material and comparing it with usage in secondary sources and with their own expectations or experiences. We expected that they could understand distinctions among given, shared, and new knowledge based on their own experience with analyzing language use. We expected they would begin to see ways that language use can reflect cultural currents. We thought that the topic itself—a hot one, provocative, and ideologically marked for issues of power—might evoke in keyboard composition the kind of "natural" style or idiolect obtained by linguists asking people to tell an important story, such as a scary experience.

In *Stories, Community and Place*, Johnstone describes how both storytellers and audience must shift together from the here-and-now of the conversation to the there-and-then of the story (Johnstone 1990:22, 30). A similar shift was necessary for conference participants in the early nineties. Drawing on ethnomethodological categories from Hymes (1972), often summarized under the mnemonic of SPEAKING, we examined the setting and scene and the participants, to see if there were any features that could have affected the students' construct of themselves as writers and as audience. (These categories include situation and scene, participants, ends, act sequence, key, instrumentality, norm, genre.) Therefore, we will first look more closely at these categories and then turn to ways the software and conference prompts set up additional challenges keyed to wrinkles in time and space.

Nearly all the participants on both campuses were students in arts and sciences: junior and senior English majors or minors, and occasional first-year graduate students in the curriculum for English as a second language. While each group used the mainframe software program VAXNotes, running on an invisible Digital VAX/VMS mainframe, the route of access to the program differed on each campus. This may have intensified the notion of "we"-ness distinguishing each campus. Although the two campuses belong to the same university system and were only ninety miles apart, they have their own attributes, both real and mythological. In the thirty years since the original Sit-Ins, the Charlotte campus has grown from a city college into a comprehensive urban university now establishing Ph.D. degrees, primarily in the professions, to serve its rapidly increasing metropolitan population. The Greensboro campus has changed from a liberal arts university for women to a coeducational university with a range of Ph.D. degrees in both the liberal arts and professions. Older residents of the state still occasionally slip and refer to the Greensboro campus as Woman's College.

Though admissions standards vary but slightly, prospective students continue to see each campus as being different in both orientation and student-body ability.

The Charlotte students were nomads, who wandered across campus, appropriating terminals in the labs found in buildings normally reserved for students in disciplines other than their own, such as engineering or business. Unless they made specific arrangements with their peers, they had no face-to-face contact with each other when keyboarding, and no support from lab assistants, who were positioned to assist with features of programs analyzing numerical data for engineering or financial applications, but not for mainframe text processing. Nomads had to know the name of their mainframe, as the Charlotte network linked several different ones. Mainframes, labs with terminals, and printers linked to the mainframe were dispersed across campus; printers were seldom found in the labs, so lab assistants had no way to assist students with print functions.

The Greensboro students were cottagers, who could and frequently did go in small groups or as a class, to the microcomputer lab at the center of the brick and cement pathways leading to the heart of the campus. Although usually more familiar with programming and financial applications than with conference applications for text processing, the lab assistants tried to assist with the VAXNotes program and could instruct students in using the range of printers available in the central lab. This microcomputer lab adjoined the mainframe cluster and supported independent text-processing as well as connections to other systems including BITNET and the Internet. In essence, the nomads' access was decentralized, with vectors pointing the students outward; the cottagers' access was centralized, with vectors pointing the students inward.

Accessing the conference: The challenge of spaces

Before reaching the text and the directions for the conference, students had to confront a number of small but important challenges, each of which framed the experience for them: finding an empty seat and a working terminal or microcomputer in a lab on their particular campus; logging onto the correct mainframe; accessing the correct software program; and accessing the correct conference.

Here they found more than one kind of prompt or frame waiting for them: the teacher-constructed directions for the full conference, the individual newspaper texts, the layout of the conferencing program itself, and comments or replies written to any topic by another student.

Though minimal, the teacher-prompt was disingenuous; we repeat it from chapter 1:

> The ARTICLE conference is a collection of newspaper articles taken from the beginning of the period of the sit-ins. Please read and respond to a minimum of four notes. Pay particular attention to the shades of meaning in verbs, modifiers, titles and honorifics.

The prompt specified a minimum number of responses in order to give students practice in using the keyboard and in becoming familiar with the software program. However, it also gave the students a chronological, hence historical, reference point and a textual characterization: the conference consisted of a series of reproduced articles from (the Charlotte and Greensboro) newspapers during the first month of the Sit-Ins. Students were thus told indirectly that the texts would be ideologically marked for crisis and confrontation between two races.

The teacher-prompt was an indirectly expressed directive, which asked students to browse and reply to any four of the texts, paying particular attention to verbs, modifiers, and ritualized or formulaic language usage. This entailed that at least one reply by each student would come from that student's reading of a newspaper text, and intended that at least one reply would present that student's reaction to the impact of word choices made by contemporary journalists. Students could not write a reply to the teacher-prompt: we disabled this alternative so that the directions would stand alone and un-modified, a permanent frame for the newspaper stories and their replies. Instead, they could access, read, and prepare to reply to text in either of two ways. By hitting the carriage-return key after reading the teacher-prompt, they could automatically enter or access the first newspaper article, which was first in both time and space. Subsequent taps of the carriage-return key would move sequentially through the entire collection of topics—texts and replies—ordered serially by topics and chronologically within each topic. Alternatively, the students could type the command DIR/ALL, which furnished an on-screen directory of numbered topics, with decimal subcategorization for replies already written "to" a particular topic's text. Students could type the number of a topic to access a primary text (the newspaper article), or the topic number, a decimal point and a subheading number (for example, 5.24) to access a secondary text (a student reply).

Space and time in the arrangement of conference texts

What the VAXNotes conferencing program calls *Topics* can be anything one wishes. In the Sit-Ins conference, the topics were the texts that we arranged spatially in relation to the direction-prompt created by the teacher and temporally in terms of the order in which the texts originally appeared in the newspapers to report the events in realtime. We set up each newspaper text as a different topic so that the spatial organization and the ordering of texts in the directory and in the order of texts in the conference would replicate the temporal order of events as they had occurred thirty years previously. The first newspaper article was both first in chronological ordering at the time of the Sit-Ins and the first topic in the listing in the directory for all the topics in the conference. Students could enter the conference through the frame of any primary (newspaper) or secondary (student-generated) text. Roughly half preferred to initiate their comings and goings with the first topic. If there were more than ten replies already submitted for a topic, these students usually read through five to eight replies before writing a response, to judge by their repetition of key words or phrases, their emulation of larger patterns, or by their direct address to specific writers. Another half apparently began by browsing the directory of topics, entering through a different topic or its appended replies. However, there were additional challenges that the students now confronted.

A second challenge for the students was their passage from their computer lab in the *now*-time of the nineties to the *then*-time of the sixties, which could be seen as an epoch, an era, a period, a decade, or as the specific week and day on which the Sit-In was reported. Notions of time were further complicated by the time in which the student was reading on the screen, writing a reply, re-membering personal experience or previous texts, constructing a gist, planning and staging (to whatever degree) the forthcoming writing, doing the writing, choosing to save the writing, and so forth.

Our time-divisions for the setting and scene presented in the newspaper texts were meant to suggest what the students apparently shared as a common context for interpreting the events reported in these stories, as we have reconstructed it from their comments in their writings. By epoch, we mean that students assigned the events to the twentieth century; by era, the era of the Vietnam war. By period, we mean the slippery and connotative construct with which students in the nineties surrounded the sixties. Whether as stereo-type or projection, certain elements seemed to reoccur as touch-stones: allusions and "quotations" from nineties raps, MTV videos, television reruns of *Saturday Night Live*'s satires, movies and co-medic monologues, and commercials featuring sixties music. These media-based references pointed to their construct of the sixties as a time of emotion and confrontation, which included: the assassina-tions of a president and major citizen-leaders; the development of an unpopular war; student revolts coupled with recreational drug use; major changes in popular music; self-consciousness about an emerging, globally-based youth culture; a cluster of ideas and ideals about race relations; and the role of news media and the press. The impact of visual media is clear, since students reported having formed their "picture" of the sixties from television and film. Students often reported that parents seldom had talked much about this period. The newspaper articles in our conference were usually the first primary source from the period that most of the students were conscious of having encountered.

The impact of realigned times and settings on monitor screens

VAXNotes, the mainframe conferencing software, stacked two sets of days and times on some of the screens it presented students, altering conventional ways of framing time. The first screen for the newspaper text initiating each topic presented the year, month, and day from the sixties for that newspaper story. On the top right of that screen, and on the first screen of all conference replies, the software provided a masthead noting the year, month, day, and time that the text was posted to the conference.

Time of day for publication of the events reported in each article was indirectly suggested by the name of the newspaper. Both Charlotte and Greensboro had morning and afternoon papers in the sixties, with slightly different titles. However, students would need to have known this fact from hearsay, memory, or prior experience, as there were usually no clues in the text to the time of day the story was distributed to homes or sold on the street. The texts themselves referred to the approximate time of day for events reported. Students frequently skipped over details about day, time, or year, and often, in their first and even second entries, wrote responses that indicated they thought an article was reporting current-day events of the nineties. We have thought about this, and have asked students about it: they report that they found themselves caught up in the narrative of the text, the story "felt like" it "could be happening today," or they simply passed by signals of "real" time and space without noticing them. Part of the blur they felt may have been caused by the ways the text was entered and the way that frames were stacked.

Each Notes-Topic in VAXNotes was a separate and complete extract from either the *Charlotte Observer*, the *Charlotte News*, the *Greensboro Daily News*, or the *Greensboro Record*. Each extract was a "story:" it was what the reporters or editors for that day's issue of that day's paper thought to be a full narrative of events that had just occurred. Each of the narrative texts had a beginning, middle, end, and title. Most, but not all, carried the by-line of the reporter who filed the "story," a decision made by the newspaper staff at the time. Each newspaper narrative reported on slightly different events: a series of confrontations, most involving students from predominantly black educational institutions in Greensboro and Charlotte with downtown businesses providing eating facilities. Students from other institutions, student leaders, and other members of black and white groupings were also mentioned. Not all of the stories or their titles dealt with the actual sit-ins, marches, or confrontations over eating. Some were narratives of other events occurring on the same day featuring other confrontations between black and white citizens, and these confrontations were overtly linked in the narrative to the sit-ins and student confrontations, either by the reporter or by the reported or quoted statements of contemporary participants.

The fact that the narratives appeared on screen instead of on paper doubtless has additional implications. The list below indicates features of the new context and situation in which the students found themselves:

- The texts could not be physically touched in the same way they could be touched in their original publication (which was not necessarily their original form): that is, one could not clip them, or do anything to or with the medium in which they appeared.
- The lettering was larger than that of the actual newspaper and its visibility was homogenous, with no variation in the ink or the font.
- The graphic pointing provided by the original medium was absent, with no headlines in large point size, boldface, or reduced type, and no expanse of surrounding white space.
- The text was in full-screen, pagelike paragraphs, with the same paragraphing as in the original, but line-length was not identical. The first screen carried a header for title, the name of conference topic and the day, month, and time the text was saved and recorded.
- The newspaper layout of head and columns was not present: there were no related stories or pictures on the same screen, nor could the reader split the screen vertically while reading to access other "stories" for parallel readings.
- The text appeared in green, orange, or white against black, as opposed to black type on white background, with or without color graphics, and the text, if touched, could not rub off on the fingers. There was no smell.
- The second screen of the text was presented in a scroll that did not stand still until the full screen was present: the lettering moved.
- The screen provided a catch phrase to tell the reader when to access the next screen. Pressing the return or enter key on the computer keyboard was not equivalent to turning a page, though it may have had the same "feel" as a kind of electronic page-turning. Just as notions of time and space begin

to blur in the electronic landscape, notions of length are distorted: a fairly short story in reduced-point type within a single column takes up a sizeable number of screens. Length became equated with time.

In essence, then, the newspaper story initiating each topic was decontextualized not only from the original appearance and format at the time of publication, but also from any other news stories and topics in the conference, unless a student called up the directory, read the titles, and entered the correct numbers in order to read a chosen newspaper story (topic) or a particular student reply. The newspaper story headlines, which we used as the "titles" for the individual topics, could give student readers a sense of progress through time. However, the factors we note here had the impact of simultaneously distancing the student from connected narratives while forcing the student to bring memory and a projected "shared knowledge" to the text being read. Students reported in post-conference analyses that the initial back-and-forth movement through the various time frames was often disorienting.; one compared the experience to being the *Nude Descending the Staircase*. The conventional frames of time, space, and memory were present in the text and surrounded the text, but they were realigned.

The challenge of expectations about genre

To judge from comments they made about newspaper stories and newspaper writers in their conference writing, students brought expectations to the text about genres that would tell them how to read these texts. They brought the presupposition that a macrostructure will surface almost immediately in time, constrained only by the linear order of the text. Some cues were present. The headline and by-line were given, so students could assign the text to the familiar genre of newspaper story. Apparently, students in the nineties brought a shared set of presuppositions about "newspaper story" in the form of a series of should-clauses:

- Articles should be factual, with no discernable "slant" or obvious features of persuasion in topic, focus, or word choice.

- Features should have a clearly visible "stance" and focus.
- Editorials should be persuasive.

Students found their assumptions about journalistic subgenres to be challenged within the first paragraph of each text: what may have seemed "unmarked," hence nonslanted, in the sixties, was "marked" for the nineties. In each conference, a discussion of media bias had to attract several discussants in more than one Notes-Topic Section (usually at least four) before any one student writer could move to voice the notion that journalists in the sixties were writing as much from and in their time and place as the student readers of the nineties were reacting from and in their time and place. The students moved, then, from a decontextualized reading of a past they did not know in detail to a recontextualized reading of their own present. This process prompted the students then to recontextualize the time and space of the past so that they were related to the present of the students' view (Ochs 1990).

The teacher-prompt directed students to examine features of word-choice such as verbs, modifiers, titles, and honorifics. Students carried a directive for some kind of content analysis to their initial readings of text, and evidently expected to be able to approach the texts in a dispassionate manner. However, they were not able to do this. Almost all students were overwhelmed by what they viewed as slanted, even offensive, prose in what they had preconceived to be neutral and factual; almost all students were flabbergasted by their own response to information that contradicted their preconceptions or pointed to their lack of knowledge about the events; almost all students were drawn to make a personal statement about the issues behind the reported confrontation, personal in the sense of reporting feelings or autobiographical self-revelation or hearsay from others in the past (ranging from childhood to "last week," from relatives to "in my history class"). The students had to reposition themselves in relation to the events in the past; they were moving toward a different stance.

An important step in the process was learning to read the carefully worded prose of the 1960s, even if biased at times, in relation to students' view of what constituted careful and bias-free statements of the 1990s. Only after one, two, sometimes three entries in reaction to ideology and issues, could most students (over 90 percent) detach themselves from the texts and their spontaneous overflow of powerful feelings in order to examine how the texts had such an impact on them, and, perhaps, why.

Replies as new frames

The final, and probably most important, frame in the conference was the series of texts written and posted by known and unknown others who were also part of the conference. When replies were appended to a text topic, students could choose to read them before or after the newspaper narrative; unless students were the first to sign on to a particular conference topic, they were never without an accessible directory to the larger audience outside themselves. That, after all, was one of the purposes of setting up the conference: to insure that students' comments would find a context, and might thereby develop some sense of common ground, even of community. Most of their writing was addressed to their peers, either directly or indirectly. Students could browse reply-titles and type the number of a particular reply they wished to read. They could append their own reply at any point in their reading, either of a newspaper story or of a student-generated reply, by typing the command "reply." The program then shifted them to a different scene in the now familiar setting of the monitor.

When the software program received the reply-command, it split the screen horizontally, so that only seven lines of the text being read could be seen and reread by the student. This constraint meant, in practical terms, that the student had to create, store, and remember a gist of the on-screen text, including whatever feature(s) had triggered the decision to reply, in terms of what the student might have already decided or planned to write. At the outset of the reply-mode, the program prompted the student writer to save the writing with a designated keystroke; hitting this key started a prompted process listed at the bottom of the screen, which titled, saved, and appended the newly written text.

The student writers were doubly constrained by space and by time. They could not rewrite or edit their text entries at a later time; once their writing was stored by VAXNotes, it became a permanent part of the conference and accessible to all participants. During the process of writing a reply, students could edit only minimally, and were typically limited to using a delete key. Their replies scrolled down a new, moving screen in the bottom half of the screen while a section from the original triggering text remained at the top. While students entering the conference on a modem-linked microcomputer in a lab or at home did have the opportunity to read, write a response using a word-processing program, upload it, and append it to a particular text (a rather complex process),only a few chose this option. Most chose instead to compose on the spot at a keyboard.

Initial replies by computer-intimidated novice keyboarders were seldom longer than the five to seven lines that the reply-screen initially presented: the scrolling motion was something they did not attempt to cope with until a second or even fourth entry, usually after having read a lengthy entry by another, less-intimidated student writer. The first entries by these novices typically had a series of errors shifted to the bottom of the reply, as the students were still learning to find the delete key, which appeared in different places on different keyboards. Less intimidated keyboarders were equally new to mainframes, but reported that they had little apprehension and felt more experienced, whether they were or not.

The first-draft nature of the rapidly composed replies forced the student to concentrate on the here-and-now for the initial writing. The student had to compose and type the reply, hit a sequence of keys to save it, and then enter a title before choosing whether to save or not save. Only then could the student return to the text originally being read. Should the mainframe belch, slow down, or suspend operations, the student had no transparent way of knowing whether the reply was saved, and momentarily lost the abilities to "read" the screen and locate the prompts, or to access the directory to see if the reply were appended. Novices worried about whether their reply was saved; even though the program sent them a confirmation, they did not recognize it as such because it was written in "computerese," a register new to them. Students were presented with shifting notions of time and space; the register of the software program's prompts and the layout of text on the screen presented additional challenges. Conference participants could get momentarily stuck in any of them. Intrigued by the possibilities of communicating with each other in this new medium, most disentangled themselves by the second or third foray.

4:// Titles: Form and function in electronic discourse

Discourse in electronic conferences is written text, the writing of which may be seen as performance and from which we may infer features of importance to and about the performers. With linear text, one knows where to begin: with the first temporal and spatial entry. However, the participants in a computer-supported conference can literally begin anywhere, entering the conference at any topic or with any individual posting. "Beginning" has a double meaning, depending on whether the conference participant is functioning primarily as a reader or as a writer. In the corpus of the "Sit-Ins" conferences, the participants usually began in their role of reader: they accessed the conference and either landed serendipitously in a text or, more usually, they typed the command DIR (for directory) to access the master list of titles, from which they typed the number of a title that interested them in order to retrieve its text. In the directory, they met a double array of titles, for each topic carried the title of the original newspaper story and the replies by other students presented student-composed titles. Students accessing the conference after its first day could choose an entry-point by either set of titles. By the number of student titles appended, the students could also assess which topics had already evoked response. They could flock to these topics or choose new ones.

Titles presented topics in their most general sense. We think the titles also afforded some notion of the language socialization processes at work in the conference. In this chapter, we look at the form and function of student-composed titles in electronic conference discourse. They are greetings for readers, closings for writers, and they play multiple roles. Titles in electronic conference discourse are

53

signposts to information and interaction. They can index speech acts of direct address, evaluation, persuasion, or disclosure, or signal the presence of reflexive language. They can suggest genres such as abstracting, reportage, argument, or challenge. They can hint at the writers' awareness of audience, by the ways they signal assent to or dissent from a peer's writing or by presenting headlines of claims and feelings. Once a title is posted, the presentation of such signals is tacitly sanctioned unless a challenge arises in another title.

Titles can suggest the epistemological perspective of the writer. The reader can then use the title as a predictive strategy for reading and as a location in memory for retention and recall when moving to write. It is not hard to locate the signpost in electronic conference discourse. What is difficult is deciding the direction in which the signpost is pointing, and whether or not the signpost is misleading. In effect, we as outsiders needed to be able to read the "map" of the conference as if we lived in the territory. Since the conference was linear within topics, and nonlinear across topics, the map would need to be multidimensional. For example, one way titles in the Sit-Ins conferences suggested the social status or role of the writers may, we think, be tied to social constructs, such as that for gender, which participants brought with them to the conferences. The usual measures—frequency of reply, frequency of posting, number of postings, number of challenges, often used to determine gender features and gender-cued dominance in oral conversation—are less directly applicable to the asynchronous electronic conference, where interruptions are impossible and where, if one tires of reading a posting, one simply exits without displaying rudeness.

For the Sit-Ins conferences, we had stipulated a minimum frequency of reply and number of postings, so we could not use frequency in ways that researchers looking at electronic mail forums might (Cooper and Selfe 1990). That is, we could not use the minimum times females or males logged on and wrote. The class assignment, in effect, eliminated the privilege to either gender. We looked next at maximums, and found that proportionally as many females as males in each class over all conferences were likely to participate more extensively than the minimum: on average, 25 percent of both male and female students in all conferences wrote more entries than the minimum stipulated. Instead of time measured by frequency of response, then, we were limited in our analysis of interaction among the student writers to intertextual references, and to a combination of internal and external reconstructive acts that drew on both time and space.

We chose six ways to examine conference titles and their accompanying postings. We reviewed all titles for every student entry in all topics of each conference: this gave us a synchronic snapshot of the ways titles served as greetings as well as closings. Next, we reviewed for interaction over time in a single notes-topic section of a conference, titles suggested how and what the writers might signal in their titles as the topic section continued, with the postings as confirmation or disconfirmation. To see if the greetings by the earliest writers in a conference might have similarities, we compared the titles and postings for the first entry in every topic across a conference. Then, we looked specifically at gender cues presented by titles, by examining all titles and postings that were written by males as a subset of all titles and all postings by all males and all females. To see whether students were emulating each other across conference topics, we examined the possibility of hypertextual linkages among titles by comparing the titles across time and across topics of all students who had come into contact with one particular student's writing. Finally, because we had varied the social setting for the participants by changing the conference from single to dual campus participation. we looked at whether students on one campus directed titles (and postings) to those on another.

One finding held true across each examination: that individuals devised their own patterns for titling; using and reusing these patterns for each posting, they often signaled features of their idiolectal preferences with their last phrase written, their title, and the first that would be read by their peers.

The impact of conference topography

The mainframe conferencing software we used, VAXNotes, is hierarchically organized. Each specific conference, called a notebook, includes separate "topics." In the Sit-Ins conference, each topic section also served as a prompt for interaction with text, whether by reading or writing. These topics served as divisions in a notebook, acting as subtopics under a main topic. The reader/writer used the conference directory-command (DIR) to access a taxonomy, numbered and dated sequentially and chronologically. However, since the reader could enter at any point in the conference, move to a subsequent entry with the carriage return key, jump to any other entry by typing its unique number, or return to the directory to jump to a new place in the conference, VAXNotes also presented the reader with some of the features of a hypertext or network. As Bolter comments, "In place of hierarchy, we have a writing that is not only topical: we might also call it "topographic" [it is] a writing with places, spatially realized topics" (1991:25).

The topography in an electronic conference allows the reader/writer to sort postings by date, writer, or title. The titles serve at least two functions: interaction and information. While we have found that students' full postings included similar discourse patterns as well as individuation and variation across the corpus, the titles of their postings showed variation and individuation within certain parameters. Like subject-headers in electronic mail, the title is part of the first text seen; unlike electronic mail, it is the last text written. Titles, like newspaper headlines, have indexical functions in that they suggest to the reader the needed macrorhetorical strategies needed for what Sidner calls focusing, by which the reader can predict and confirm or disconfirm things about the text (Sidner 1983; Faigley 1985, 1986). Van Dijk's work with text linguistics during 1980 to 1985 included an examination of different aspects of news stories as part of his work with "schematic superstructures . . . the conventional global form of a discourse" (van Dijk 1985: 155). He notes that the headline and lead are "conventional forms that characterize a specific discourse genre" (158). Like headlines, the titles for postings in electronic conference discourse have conventional form and indexical function.

Based on her comparison of headlines in an eminent newspaper, *The Times of London,* with a popular tabloid, *The Daily Mirror,* Ingrid Mardh (1980) found four types of headlines: statements, questions, commands, and explanations. Different newspapers develop stylistic preferences as to functional type, typographical features, even linguistic features such as an abundance of adverbial or nominal clauses in the headlines. Lexicon plays a role as well (Mardh 1980:11–13).

Drawing on Mardh's comparison between *The Times* and *The Daily Mirror*, or from any pairing between a newspaper priding itself on the quality, dependability, and prestige of its reporting, and a tabloid priding itself on the quality, dependability, and prestige of its sensational appeal to readers, we would expect different sets of headlines about an alleged bombing during the Sit-Ins. For example, a tabloid might use a headline and subheads such as these:

DAY OF TERROR

POLICE THRONG TO SURROUND ARMY OF MARCHERS

THREAT OF BOMB TERRIFIES HELPLESS SHOPPERS

The actual newspaper headline and subhead from February 7, 1960, was:

BOMB SCARE SCATTERS 400 AT DIME STORES

In other words, headlines and titles present cues to the reader about what to expect. Readers understand these headlines and titles in terms of the publication's typical register, which is part of the publication's historical context.

These cues may be somewhat skewed in electronic conferencing. The titles of the topics in the Sit-Ins conference were the first seven words of the headlines to the original stories appearing in Feburary-March 1960. Unlike regular headlines, however, they gave minimal clues to the reader because their style was not as florid as a tabloid's, and the on-screen typed format could not present form, size, position, or font as cues to the reader. The headlines of newspapers, like the titles taken from them in the Sit-Ins conference are a type of "display language," having what Halliday and Hasan (1976) called an "economy grammar," or they may be termed "block language" (Quirk, Greenbaum, Leech, and Svartvik 1972:414–15). Included in this category are labels, telegrams, and tabulated text such as catalogues. Characteristic features include dependent clauses used independently, noun phrases with stacked modification, and the absence of definite articles and the copula. Many of these features surfaced in the student-composed titles.

Titles furnished by the student writers in the conferences were such a "block language," and shared many of the features of headlines, particularly in their economy of grammar. The students' titles often evoked direct emulation of other titles and their functions. For example, they could indicate audience awareness on the part of the writer by specifying that an individual posting was a response directed to another writer, another posting, or to a previous posting by the author. Titles could be used as blazons, presenting the name of the writer, or they might highlight affect or be directed to a more general readership. Titles were seldom innocuous, though they may have been phatic in the sense developed by Cheepen (1988) in her study of interaction in informal conversation.

Cheepen noted that as ethnomethodologists have worked with interaction, their focus has been on the management of discourse, for which topic placement is crucial. Aspects of conversational analysis such as "side sequence" or "repair," she noted, imply the larger notion of topic. Phatic conversation, she claimed, is often misinterpreted by linguists, but is more than a filler, since phatic communion—one of the three functions of language delineated earlier by Malinowski—is interactional language, important for what Cheepen called interactional encounters.

Student-composed titles were a doorway to interaction and interactional encounters. As the earliest cue the reader received, the title supported the building of an interactional electronic community. That is, they presented aspects of status in the sense that they often indexed the gist of a posting, or suggested its illocutionary force, including the writer's stance toward readers. Like the postings they headed, titles were complex in the ways they presented given, new, inferrable, and shared information. They spilled over with repetition, and suggested norms of politeness for ways the writers referred to or replied to each other.

Van Dijk and Kintsch (1983: 9) have commented that "There is no unitary process of comprehension, but variable comprehension processes in different situations, of different language users, of different discourse types." Our corpus extends to electronic discourse their claim that titles are an important part of the reader's notion of the macrostructure of a text. That is, the user's guesses or predictions about the text will frame the user's reading strategy. These predictions will derive from "titles, thematic words, thematic first sentences, knowledge about possible ensuing global events or actions, and information from the context" (van Dijk and Kintsch 1983:15–16). Each successive conference presented the students with a slightly different social context in terms of whether the participants were in classes on a single campus or in a linkage of classes on separate campuses. Comparing the titles allowed us to infer how the students handled issues of situation.

We analyzed all the titles in the Stand Alone and Transparent conferences and for the first three topics of the Exchange conference. In the Stand Alone conference, students at each campus were presented with identical prompts within identical software packages, and saw only the writings of students on their own campus: two different classes at UNCC wrote in one conference and one class at UNCG wrote in the other. In the Transparent conference, students in two classes at UNCC and one at UNCG were presented with one set of prompts mounted on one mainframe and running on both campus mainframes simultaneously. We assessed norms by comparing these two conferences, which had minimal interference from the instructors but took place in different virtual settings.

For the Exchange conference, students in a single class at each campus were presented with identical prompts within identical software packages. Each class knew that the other class was reading and responding to the same prompts and that their completed conference writing would be sent to the other campus. At the close of the conference, instructors saved the full conference as a file and shipped it to the mainframe on the other campus. Each class was then presented with the full conference composed at the other campus, and prompted to respond at least twice within it, though the nature of their response was not directed. Since response was enjoined to prompts already familiar and direct address was indirectly supported by the notion of an exchange, the count of their patterns during the second stage of their conference skews the analysis of expected conventions that would arise without intervention of the instructor. We limited our detailed examination to the first three topics of the Exchange conference, since those three topics drew the heaviest response for both the first and the second stage of the conference. Students received the conference from the other class near the end of the semester; unless they had a particular interest in a later topic from their previous experience in their own conference, they tended to sign on to the conference, access one of the first three topics, browse the writings by students, and post responses.

In essence, the first stage of the Exchange conference replicated the interaction of the Stand Alone. The second stage, when writers had some expectation of being read by students on the other campus, was more like the Transparent. Hence our decision to compare the Stand Alone and Transparent conferences for titling conventions.

Conventions of direct address in titles

Titles that clearly indicated that they were a reply or response to a text or writer in the conference used these patterns, in order of occurrence:

Reply to article-number
Reply to person, addressed by name or user id
Reply to title of Article (in Notes-Topic Section), which may be
    truncated
Reply to title of text by another writer in the conference
Reply with no text or audience specified.

Because a student might read posting 3.37 and compose a reply to it did not mean that the student's reply was indexed as 3.38: if other writers had entered text after 3.37 was written, the reply was indexed by the software as any number after the topic-numeral: 3.38, 3.56, and so forth. Hence students usually signaled the text to which their response "belonged" if they intended, consciously or otherwise, for the next reader to understand a "given" context for their posted response.

Students used these patterns of wording to indicate direct address, in order of occurrence:

Reply to X
Response to X
Reply/response to X
Re: X
To X

Reply/response X [no "to"]
X reply/response
Agree with/disagree with/cheers to/understand X

As our comparison of the Stand Alone and Transparent conferences shows, direct address was present in student titles, but was not prevalent.

Use of these patterns was tied to student notions of conventions for direct address in the "home community" and to their willingness to target specific prompts or persons with a signal in the title. Direct address in a title may have seemed impolite, rash, or rude, similar to flaming in electronic mail or discussion lists. In Internet discussion lists, writers in 1993 to 1995 who were writing anything other than a question directed to all readers on the list, usually cited the previous posting and its author/cognomen, included a quotation from that posting, and directed their response simultaneously directly to that posting and to the list in general, since writers knew their postings are public.

What has been called "flaming" in electronic lists, a public challenge and disagreement, usually negative in tone and sometimes typed in all-capital letters, could range from the equivalents of a raised voice to shouted insults. Student writers in mainframe electronic conferences, however, were often hesitant to express

Table 4.1. How students varied direct address

Conference	Total Writings	Addressed Named Person ("Go Sandy")	Addressed Writings by Notes Topic Number ("To 2.11")	Addressed Article by Title ("Reply to Works")	Addressed Directions ("Response to 'Verbs'")
Stand Alone					
UNCC	161	5	1	5	6
UNCG	97	9	34	5	3
Total	258	14	35	10	9
Transparent (UNCG & UNCG)					
Total	229	7	19	4	5

outright disapproval of or disagreement with other writers, and directed such to the writings instead.

Why were the students hesitant? They knew we were dropping in and reading the postings; perhaps this contributed to their restraint. Some were hesitant about their ability to compose at the keyboard and self-conscious about typographical errors; others remained uneasy with the log-on and access routines and with finding and entering the conference. Perhaps they were not quite sure that we sincerely meant that we would neither interfere, intervene, or "grade" their writings beyond checking to see that they had posted something; they may not have been confident that it really was a closed conference until they had monitored it (and us) over time. Then, too, the students did not know everyone in the face-to-face classes and, though they had a printed list of userids and corresponding student names, they seldom referred to either. Timing within a conference played a role as well. It was often not until either five entries on a particular topic had been posted, or until the second entry by any individual writer that acts of self-disclosure or disagreement with a peer, became typical. Instead of signaling direct address, the titles often suggested that personal response or disclosure would be found within the entries.

Titles as suggestive of self-disclosure

Acts of self-disclosure ranged over a continuum, from some minimal evaluation of events narrated in the newspaper story to lengthy autobiographical narrative and statements of personal feeling. Titles were most often used to signify to the assumed reader the amount of personal involvement they might expect to find, such as revelation of reaction-to-text, disclosure of personal feelings and personal life story, or evaluation of text, its issues, and its posted replies. Direct replies were enfolded within this continuum.

Most of the titles did not include words such as reply (to), respond. They signaled readers in other ways:

—appropriation of part or all of the text-prompt as a title: *Bomb scare;*
—appropriation of part or all of another student's title: *Frustration: more;*

—a new phrase or clause with one or more words quoted from the original headline: *Hero marches*;

—a phrase or clause citing a topical concept, usually as a synonym, from the newspaper story: *Woolworth's problem*; *Doctors stymied*;

—a phrase or clause of personal feeling: *Frustrated*;

—a phrase or clause combining word or topical concept with word(s) that could imply affective or evaluative content: *Racist again*; *To serve or not to serve*; *Woolworth, Would We Have Done the Same?*

In Table 4.2, QT means that the title quoted, paraphrased, or alluded to a specific text. PF means that the title presented some suggestion of personal feeling, disclosure, or stance. CPF was a title combining reference to a text with some notion of feeling or disclosure. PN was a title that referred to another text by its number only. DIR included titles that referred in some way to the directions for the conference. OWN was a title that included some form of the writer's own name, including first or last name, nickname, or initials.

The heavy use of QT titles in the UNCG Stand Alone conference was due, the instructor thought, to students' carryover of directions from one part of their previous computer training, in which they had learned to copy the title of a previous entry. The titles for the UNCG

Table 4.2. How Titles Referred

Conference	QT	PF	CPF	PN	DIR	OWN
Stand Alone						
UNCC	27	19	19	19	7	27
UNCG	97	35	1	4	4	2
Transparent	40	7	26	5	1	132

Note: QT = the title quoted, paraphrased, or alluded to a specific text
PF = the title presented some suggestion of personal feeling, disclosure, or stance
CPF = a title combining reference to a text with some notion of feeling or disclosure
PN = a title that referred to another text by its number only
DIR = titles that referred in some way to the directions for the conference
OWN = a title that included writer's own name, including first or last name, nickname, or initials

portion of the Exchange conference replicated the patterning of the UNCC Stand Alone conference. What seemed significant was the heavy use of OWN titles in the Transparent conference, which mixed both campuses simultaneously. The total number of student postings in the two Stand Alone conferences was 161 postings; 29 student titles, or 18 percent, used the writers' names. The total number of postings in the Transparent conference was 228, with 132 titles bearing the name of their writers: 57 percent. Something was being signaled.

If we consider titles as a form of greeting, variety was apparently sanctioned. We did not find emulation across the chronological order of entries; we did, however, find individuals establishing and in later entries, keeping to their preferred patterns, beginning with the first titles they assigned. When we looked at the full set of titles used by each person throughout the whole conference, some patterns surfaced for the group as a whole, for gender cohorts, but in general patterns were individually established and maintained by the writers. For example, the male writers neither used initials nor quotation marks in their titles; proportionally, however, they were no more likely than women to use variations on the *Reply-to-X* formula in their titles. Women occasionally used another student's name in a direct-address title, but were more likely to use content-bearing words from the newspaper headline or from another student's title, such as <*reply to white owners 10.2*>. The only males who presented direct-address titles such as <*Reply to Carter*> were older by a range of two to twenty years than the mean age (twenty years) of the classes and from outside the region; perhaps they felt outnumbered, or that it would be somehow impolite to reply directly to a name.

Students often used titles as a way of summing up their entries. The impact was that the titles could present slight clues to readers as to the degree of affect or disclosure the reader was likely to find, which indirectly sanctioned such discourse acts. In the Stand Alone and Exchange conferences, titles were not used for emulation or for "play" in the ways they were used in the titling game of the Transparent conference.

The titling game and its impact

A few students in each conference had chosen to number their responses to signal their completion of the task—for example, "Response 1/First Reply." Others titled their responses with their name, nickname, or initials: none used their user id as a way to refer to themselves. Titles involving personal first names or nicknames, synonyms for "say," "think," and occasional alliteration became a game that wove throughout the Transparent conference. The game began with a small group of the first students to respond in the conference on one campus (UNCC), with titles such as "Sam speaks," "Connie comments," "Kenya adds," "Penny ponders," and was picked up by students from the other campus once they signed on.

Several aspects of this game were especially interesting. First, students on both campuses sustained the game throughout all of topic 2 in the Transparent conference, the initial topic and the one that drew the greatest number of responses, and resumed the game at intervals throughout the remaining topics of the conference. Next, it added an element of word play to a conference focusing on language in a "hot" and humorless context. While the titles occasionally one-upped each other as one or another student presented a new word to signal personal commentary, the responses were generally incisive and serious. That students used their first names or nicknames, and continued the titling formula throughout the conference suggests an effort to involve audience through personalizing titles. The element of word play carried over into titles keyed to the prompts but with an aphoristic element, such as "To Serve or not to serve: Woolworth." Table 4.3 illustrates the titling game, with the first fifteen titles and a summary of themes in their accompanying postings from topic 8, which attracted 60 percent of the students.

Students did not use their userids for this additional, often playful layer of discourse. The userids were created on each campus by different programs. The UNCC student userid used the formula ENONXXX, where EN identified the student as taking an English class, ON was the section number, and XXX was the set of initials for the student's legal full name. The UNCG student userid was six to eight characters long, usually a combination of letters from the student's first and last name, and unique in the campus computer system. A UNCG student could immediately recognize the identity of most of the other UNCG students from the userid, particularly since the UNCG classes were smaller and had practiced using the system for an earlier assignment in a microcomputer lab connected to the mainframe and the software program. UNCC students had less personal contact and their ids were personalized only by the

Figure 4.3. The Titling Game

Student identification:
Ca = Charlotte class section 1   Cb = Charlotte class section 2   G = Greensboro class

Entry	Title	Address	Summary of "story"
[200: Newspaper story: "Aid Given"]			
201 Cb-1	Spud speaks	uses first name, speech-act verb	— personal reaction, empathy for protestors
202 CB-2	Nora speaks too	echoes Spud's verb, use of first name	— journalism slanted, echoes teacher prompt to introduce word choice analysis "orderly, jeering, nigger, burr-head" — issues of tone, journalism practiced in the 60s
203 Ca-1	Donna's turn	uses first name, names speech act	— agrees, assessment of situation, not on style, agree on tone in that time/place ("relative to its historical context") "I agree with Spud and Nora.... However, in response to Nora's observation.... I DO agree with Nora's observation that...."
204 Ca-2	Sondra responds	speech-act verb, first name	— reports with "we like" the attitudes of her home country/culture — issue: businessmen had social contract
205 Cb-3	Karla 1	first name; personal posting number	— identifies self as exchange student, query regarding businessmen, empathy/support for protestors
206	Crawford	first name	— title empathy "some surprise, similar to Nora's...."

Code	Title	Feature	Description
Cb-4			— issues of journalistic bias, role of titles
207 Ca-3	Woolworth's memories	[memories of Woolworth's]	— childhood memories from 60s did not include racism; introduces notion of foreigners as instigators
208 Cb-4	Crawford adds	speech-act verb, first name	— corrects, expands word choice analysis in 206 "as Sondra so wisely noted"
209 Cb-5	tne 3	initials, personal posting number	— locates self as born after events, personal history; stands up for "foreigner"
210 Ca-4	Allie speaks	speech act verb (201), first name	— correlates with lit class study of novel; specific word choice "Negro" "Donna, I agree with you … also agree with you when you say…." — agrees on issues of empathy, journalistic context keyed to place
211 Cb-6	answered 1d	speech-act nominalized posting sequence (a–d)	— emotion in article; evaluates article "I, too, agree with Nora and Donna"
212 G1	Ariadne's thoughts	mental-act nominalized, first name	— word choice of "nigger," disagrees indirectly—sees journalist as 'lackadaisical' and "unsympathetic"; fine tunes notion of audience for different culturally-based media
213 Ca-5	fhy 1	initials, personal posting number	— projects what s/he might have done then
214 Ca-6	Bart's reply	use of first name; specifies speech act	— theme of ignorance; cites friends, evaluates racist behavior, summarizes values
215 Ca-7	[no title]	[absence of title may suggest something]	— use of capitals to distinguish "Negro"

initials of their formal "university records" names. What both classes could recognize, however, was the formula for the userid from the other campus; they always knew, when reading a particular response, the home base of its writer.

Students in the Transparent conference did, however, use userids in their titles for replies to particular postings, which, though unsigned, always carried the userid of the author, because the software provided it on the opening screen of each entry. Occasionally double reference was used in a title: *My response to 3.14-EN03BHD* or *To "Frustrated"-BREWERJ*. The software provided and indeed enforced a variation on the memorandum format: instead of prompting the writer for a subject header before beginning to write an entry, VAXNotes required the writer to choose a title after the entry was written. The titling game, as evidencing people's play with each other's words, could arguably serve as suggestive of enculturation through emulation into tacit rules for the temporary discourse community united by its common task (see Swales 1990). We paused to consider the possible impact of the software itself on the embryonic and evolving community conventions presented by the titling game.

Managing community: Software and moderator impact

We found ourselves uneasily considering the notion that there might be something about title-driven conferencing that contributed to the formation of an ephemeral community, something different from an equally short-lived sequence of exchanges in e-mail or e-messages. The writers of titles were creating them with a duality of force: they were summing up what they had just written, perhaps giving it a final twist, while knowing their title would be the first bit of text that would invite classmates to read the writing. Their accompanying writings were not precisely letters, nor were they crafted essays. Instead, like the titles, the writings presented multiple ways of showing the writers' awareness of being in a public forum, even though the forum was limited to classmates. Our role as participant-observers in a community was blurred: we observed, but our participation was partial, being limited to the act of reading while the conference was in session. Looking at the titling game as a signal that some sort of community norms had developed became a signpost for us to look more closely at some aspects of community-formation in computer conferencing, beginning with the possible impact of the conferencing software's design.

One feature of VAXNotes software for mainframes and net-worked microcomputers had some impact on conference writing in that, as a precursor of hypertext and as an "early" type of groupware, it established the use of titles as opposed to the subject-headers of conventional e-mail formats. Jeff Jancula of Digital Equipment, in a 1993 telephone interview about the history of the VAXNotes package, commented that it began to evolve during the mid-seventies among a group of engineers working on PDP 11 systems, which were precursors of the 1990s VAX machines. By 1980, VAXNotes had been formalized. The prototype for commercial purposes was developed in 1985, field testing took place in 1987, and it was offered for sale in 1988. In 1994, one could run the product on a mainframe, to link far-flung users or to host the conference on a mainframe connected to a fileserver that serviced local area networks for desktop microcomputers. Software that promotes interaction or collaboration among multiple users was, by 1994, often called groupware.

Researchers such as Starr Roxanne Hiltz (1984), Sherry Turkle (1984), Linda Harasim (1990), and Shoshanna Zuboff (1988) have investigated the impact of computers on community-formation in business and in education for the past two decades. The focus of much current research in fields such as communications or technical writing is on issues of how a group is formed and sustained, whether the collaboration is real time (synchronous) or delayed time (asynchronous), and whether the software or groupware promotes or delays social interaction and collaborative learning. An associated and interrelated issue is that of "distributed " knowledge: here no one group member has sole and proprietary control of knowledge. It is distributed in various ways among group members. Several studies on teamwork and collaboration, such as the collection in Galegher et al. 1990, suggest how current researchers from a variety of disciplines draw on linguistic models for conversation and discourse analysis to study issues of cooperative or collaborative work in computer environments.

McGrath's (1990) study, "Time Matters in Groups," is an example of the kinds of insights that occur when the researcher seeks answers to questions important to several fields or disciplines. After establishing patterns and deriving "implicit rules" for group communications in face-to-face conversation, he reviewed various technologies that might promote or impede communications. For this list of rules, he operationalized and expanded a number of insights from conversation, speech-act and discourse analysis, such as his reformulation of the maxim of quantity in conversation (see Grice 1975). In face-to-face communications, one person has the floor and a "default" speaker is always present; permission is obtained for the next speaker to gain the floor, as floor time is shared. Transitions between speakers are signaled by multiple cues, such as pauses, which must be neither too short nor too long. Of special interest for examining interaction in electronic discourse and those of its features that are like conversation are his last four "rules": a group's members have no anonymity among themselves, assume that "no outsiders will intrude," and that any speaker will either connect speech to preceding communication or declare a new connection (McGrath 1990: 49). In the series of Sit-Ins conferences, students were not anonymous, and the conferences were closed to people outside the class. However, the way electronic discourse is dispersed throughout a conference means that cohesion among texts and cohesiveness among writers is handled in a variety of ways. The titling game was one of these ways that conference participants made connections with each other and established expectations for each other.

There is apparently a continuum of expectations for the functions that software/groupware can promote or serve, as well as a continuum for the degree to which the group interaction is "managed." At one end of the continuum is the "conversation," which needs human management. At the other end is the software itself, which presents the management factors. The Sit-Ins conferences probably fell somewhere in the middle of the continuum, because we initiated a "conversation" but instead of moderating it, allowed the software protocols to "manage" part of the interaction. For an explanation of human management, we follow Rice's discussion of the moderator (Rice 1980, Rice and Barnett 1986) as being the person who reminds, tracks, clarifies, prompts, reviews, distills, negotiates, mitigates, mediates, arbitrates. All of these acts imply a focus on a topic as the basis for the community and assume that both positive and negative politeness, from disagreement to open conflict, will be present. The moderator is, in Alan Purves's terms, the scribe (1990): the person charged with presenting and representing the record, the history and the context.

The moderator is often present in real time or synchronous conferencing, which ranges from the ENFI system, first implemented by Trent Batson for students at Gaulladet University, through a variety of software products, such as Daedalus and InterChange, that allow composition instructors to network a microcomputer laboratory or classroom, usually for real time conversational interaction through writing (see Tuman 1992a, 1992b). And it is these situations, with the instructor serving as participant as well as observer, that have sparked concerns of professionals in rhetoric and composition studies about issues of coercion and privacy in the computer writing classroom: see Schwartz (1992), or Hawisher and LeBlanc (1992).

At the other end of the continuum is the "conversation" managed by the software itself. The "In Depth" section of the computer magazine *Byte* focused its December 1988 feature on groupware, and included a discussion by linguist Terry Winograd, author of *Understanding Computers and Cognition* (1986). A key focus in Winograd's discussion of *The Coordinator* software was the way this particular software itself becomes the "manager" or "coordinator" of discussions by its users, by prompting the reader/writer to declare a conversational act before writing. The conversations enabled by *The Coordinator* are often "conversations for action": the thread or indexing feature provides the history/context for each message by specifying the act that its writer declared and the kinds of acts that are expected in return. Reciprocity, even when the act is silence, is assumed. When Denise Murray (1991) published her monograph on electronic conversation, which included insights from her earlier articles on language use in the computer environment, she used the model presented by *The Coordinator* and its developers to discuss the kinds of messages and their features that she had collected from on-line messaging at a Silicon Valley computer corporation.

The expansion of software with conferencing features to include graphics (still and moving) and numerical data suggests that it is evolving to meet additional communicative needs. Lotus Works, a groupware program to accompany the spreadsheet and database programs supported by Lotus, was developed by Ray Ozzie. It presents both synchronous and asynchronous messaging and conferencing. Like VAXNotes its conference program prompts conferees to type a title. Eileen Blanchette of the Lotus Notes team commented in a 1993 telephone interview that the conferencing system promotes collaboration on several levels for both reading and writing, and that the writing is more like formal letters than like memos or e-mail. This suggests that a difference in the kind of text produced by title-driven software is recognized and acknowledged, even if informally, by manufacturers and distributers. Letters must provide context and macrocues to the reader. Unlike the evanescent messaging or electronic mail, letters present a different kind of referentiality and cohesion: differences in indexicality would be expected. Titles in electronic conference discourse play some kind of role in providing contextual cues that writers think readers might value.

Computer conferencing was first implemented by Turoff in 1970, to be a "collective intelligence environment" (Harasim 1990:41). Harasim's collection, *OnLine Education*, included her own discussion of processes facilitated by computer conferencing: idea-generating; idea-linking, and idea-structuring (see esp. 55–56). Harasim cautioned that idea-linking is more frequently associated with convergent thinking, adding that the networks, concept maps, semantic webs, and connectivist theories of knowledge building, which have attracted so many rhetoricians to hypertext, promote divergent thinking, and are difficult to achieve in the on-line environment, which is often more linear.

We wonder whether the kinds of prompts, and the kind of conferences we study here, might allow some knowledge-building in divergent modes because of their title-driven nature. There is more going on than meets the eye in a full conference. A title-driven conference allows readers and writers to develop and use a message map, in the sense of Levin, Kim, and Riel (1990:200–201): that is, who references whom, keyed to what topics. However, because affective and illocutionary cues are so often suggested in the titles and sustained by the postings, the message map can be multidimensional. Issues of referentiality and issues of politeness, as they connect with each other, might expand our notions of what is going on in an on-line asynchronous discussion.

For especially the last decade, the interests of many linguists, communications specialists, and rhetoricians have been converging as they move to examine written text. Linguists have returned to examine reference, cohesion, register, and interaction in written text, formerly the province of historical linguists and philologists. The study of "figure," a rhetorical domain, lurks within any study of reference. Rhetoricians have been slipping quietly under the fence, dividing their examination of social interaction and audience from that of linguists: a theory of tropes often hides beneath any theory of emergence or interaction. Communications specialists have been appropriating conversation analysis, which gives them an opportunity to study reference and social interaction from yet a third viewpoint. It is almost as if, over the last twenty years, people interested in looking at the social contexts for written and oral text have quietly redisplayed themselves in ways that allow each group to preserve disciplinary autonomy while drawing on each others' findings. Recent volumes of journals such as *Language and Society*, *Written Communication*, and *Communications Yearbook* show earlier emphases on formalism met by countercurrents interested in meaning and context. All three disciplines are looking at language emergence, at interaction, conversation, and transaction. Perhaps what is needed is a new areal model of diffusion to explain why there is more to language, to writing, to reading, to conversing than labeled hierarchies. We find ourselves reminded of the quarrels surrounding the neogrammarian hypotheses about contact and change in the previous century, for when one studies the use of language in electronic communications, one must look at both the diachronic and the synchronic aspects of language.

The kinds of interactions in the computer conferences we have studied are probably most like those reported by Wilkins (1991). In her study of multiparty conversation on a conferencing network for an electronic communcations utility over a period of three months, she examined ways that the "participants used personal names and lexical referents" to establish conversation. In ordinary conversation, she notes, response would include direct address, but would not include naming. Instead, what kept conversation flowing was neither references by name or number or established conversational sequences. Instead "the conversational topic was maintained through lexical repetition, synonyms and shared cultural knowledge" (Wilkins

1991: 63). We find these features substantiated by our data. However, we also find that the postings in the title-driven conferences have resonances to other kinds of written texts, particularly letters. Here we have found Biber's computational discourse studies to be particularly helpful in understanding what and how titles in the Sit-Ins conferences were both greetings and closure.

In *Variation across Speech and Writing* (1988), Biber tagged a large number of structures in a variety of texts, and used multivariate and factor analysis on those structures in order to set up continuums that could move beyond distinguishing speech from writing to distinguish among genres, his primary concern. His goal was "to specify the multidimensional relations among the many different types of speech and writing in English" (Biber 1988: 25), as opposed to establishing an absolute or reductive distinction between speech and writing. Hence he used quantitative techniques to "identify the groups of features that actually co-occur in texts, and afterwards these groupings are identified in functional terms" (13). Biber identified a number of factors that would allow a more precise study of the dimensions characterizing spoken and written text: for example, was the text interactive or edited, abstract or situated, reported or immediate? His factor analysis enabled the charting of relationships among genres of text, spoken or written, along these dimensions.

Because student postings or replies in the Sit-Ins conferences have much in common with letters—in that they are situated, reply to a prompt, include information keyed to the prompt as well as to personal feelings or opinions, and are generally directed toward an audience—Biber's distinctions between *professional letters* and *personal letters* are particularly interesting. Biber found that "professional letters consistently have a much greater range of scores [on dimensions based on factor analysis] than personal letters, which contradicts the intuitive response that personal letters would, like conversation, be what Biber calls "unconstrained" in their linguistic form. However, personal letters in Biber's sample differed very little, keyed to their interactive and affective purposes. Professional letters, on the other hand, could mix interactional and informational purposes, which resulted in wide variation in lexical variety, informational density, and affective or interactive features, such as private verbs and present tense (Biber 1988: 131–32). In their writings, students mixed both purposes. That mixture was often suggested by their final bit of prose for each writing, the title. In their encapsulated form, titles, especially in the titling game, presented both interaction and information. Just as people thrown together in a common situation tend to proffer similar greetings to all whom they may not know well, so will they establish and maintain specific ways of titling their conference postings.

5:// Defining the territory

Speakers of a language cannot account for how they know what to do; it is probable that writers and readers cannot always account for what they do, either. The electronic discourse of our corpus gives, we think, a glimpse of some aspects of language competence through the ways its participants interact as they define their own territory or affect each other's responses, even when they are unaware of what they are doing. Since interaction in electronic conference discourse is carried on through writing, not oral conversation, they cannot modulate, for example, their tone of voice as their story gets more exciting or their sense of the territory changes, but they can modify some feature of their writing. As they change features in any part of their writing, their style shifts In this chapter, we look at some aspects underlying their shifts of style.

There are no interruptions or overlaps or granting of the floor in asynchronous electronic discourse. It is written in individual entries that are appended by the software in the order in which the writing was saved and distributed. The software also establishes how the discourse is bounded and segmented in both space and time. The face-to-face gestures, the subvocalization signals, and other features of spoken interactions are missing. That does not mean that electronic discourse is without emotion, or necessarily underprivileged in some way. Writers, like speakers, shift their styles to accommodate a number of factors. One factor, for example, is keyed to constraints from the medium or channel of communication. Another is in response to something affecting them from what they have just read. And a third factor is what they think of as "their" territory and, especially, their audience.

Bell's 1984 study "Language Style as Audience Design," described style shift as "at base a speaker's response to the audience. A speaker who takes the initiative and redefines the situation through speech is still responding to the audience" (184–85). In the multiparty interaction of an electronic conference, it is the writer who responds to audience, in ways that are fairly complex. Bell notes that speakers in an interaction can assess the personal characteristics or general style level of their audience, and possibly even "their addressee's levels for specific linguistic variables" (167).

What Bell drew from accommodation theory (Giles and Powesland 1975; Scherer and Giles 1979; Giles, Coupland, and Coupland 1991) to account for shifts of styles at the phonological level in spoken discourse may be relevant as well to the conversational writing in electronic discourse. Bell emphasized that "speakers accommodate their style to their audience" (162), with audience including the addressee, the auditor, and the overhearer (see Bell 1995). This description of audience includes the range of roles played by participants in an electronic conference in that student writers could read/"hear" texts addressed directly to them, read/"hear" texts addressed to others but feel themselves included by stylistic features in those texts, or read/"overhear" texts addressed to others. The reader, feeling a change in tone, responds to shifts in lexical diversity, which are co-occurent with syntactic features; this signals the writer's stance. But participants were more than readers in the Sit-Ins conference; they were writers as well, and the constellations of lexical and syntactic features in their writings shifted as each person's purpose, intent, content, or viewpoint for writing changed.

In this chapter, we look at several of those features and the way writers used them to establish, maintain, and shift territory and style.

Individual views of the territory

Naomi Baron (1984) may have been the first researcher to consider electronic discourse "as part of the study of human language" (124) rather than as part of the use of computers. Her communication continuum—face-to-face communication, teleconferencing, telephones, computers, and writing—focused on the spatial and temporal relationships among the participants (120). She noted that "we know almost nothing about how participants in computer conferencing compensate more generally for lack of physical presence and non-linguistic presence" (129).

Baron concluded with a discussion of the probable need for prescriptivism because she thought electronic discourse, as suggested in Isaac Asimov's novel (1957), *The Naked Sun*, could have negative consequences on both spoken and written language. However, before making predictions, it is useful to know more about what individual participants do with language in interactive electronic discourse in order to understand how they as writers "compensate" for the lack of physical cues in the medium by drawing on their own repertoire of conversational and writing features and strategies, including the ways they accommodate or adapt to the linguistic and social cues of other writers. Since electronic conference discourse is written text, whose minimal unit is the word (see Youmans 1991), an entry point into understanding the nature of and the variation in that text is the measurement of lexical diversity.

Type-token ratio (TTR) measures and quantifies lexical diversity as a particular aspect of variation in the usage by any single student writer, and by all student writers in the conference. Lexical diversity is indicated by the amount of repetition present in a text. TTR, which measures the number of different words in a text as a percentage of the total words within that text, can provide a profile of language behavior. Analyzing shifts in the amount of lexical diversity, or lexical repetition, as presented by a particular writer, can allow us to identify how writers do what they do in their discourse. The TTR marks major shifts in discourse as they are signaled by a rise or fall in the amount of lexical repetition, relative to a mean. This means of getting at the ways all writers write to each other in a multiparty discourse provides a way, then, of quantifying changes in a single writer's language behavior. We divided every writing in each of the conferences of our corpus into successive fifty-word chunks and then calculated the TTR for each segment of the text.

The TTR can be used to measure variation for an individual speaker or writer rather than for a group. It indicates the individual's variation from his or her mean. A segment with a TTR higher than the mean for that speaker's or writer's statement presents more diversity and less repetition. Changes of TTR within a speaker's or writer's discourse indicates an individual's shift in style or register by marking the changes in the level of lexical diversity.

Carpenter (1990) based his study of depositions, oral testimony, and cross-examination during a trial on earlier studies of written text as well as oral speech. In his study of tape transcripts, Carpenter found that speakers "experiencing apprehension or caution about possible adverse or negative reactions from listeners have higher TTRs than utterances that are more spontaneous when no threat is perceived" (Carpenter 1990:7).

Speakers who had good reason to be careful, lest they incriminate themselves, had higher TTRs in crucial segments of their testimony. Would writers of electronic conference discourse show a higher TTR when discussing potentially "hot" topics about race or political ideology? They did, but not in the ways one might think. TTR analysis of each writing of 150 words or longer did identify the rise and fall of lexical diversity for each individual writer, but those shifts pointed to a variety of language behaviors, since the shifts and styles differed from writer to writer.

TTR, as used by Carpenter and others (see references in Stubbs 1996:122ff.), can be used to analyze different aspects of language behavior. For example, Carpenter (1990) pointed out that analysis of the second presidential debate in 1976 showed that President Ford changed his language behavior after making his misstatement that "there is no Soviet domination of Eastern Europe." Although President Ford did not change his physical appearance, he did change his language behavior, an inward change marked outwardly by more careful and cautious use of language as the debate continued. The TTR, which provided a means of documenting this subtle but significant shift, has also been applied to the study of the texts of the speeches of all twentieth-century presidents (Carpenter 1990: 5–6). Presidential speeches are, typically, written texts presented orally in staged or carefully controlled contexts. Electronic conference discourse is written text composed at the computer keyboard and then presented in visual rather than printed form. Initially, the two would seem very different; there is, however, a commonality between these two kinds of texts.

The students' writing performances had multiple functions. The individual segments of their texts shifted, relative to the writers' means, from lower to higher TTRs, or from higher to lower TTRs, depending on their purposes—to deal with apprehension, to cooperate with other student writers in creating a discourse community, to protect themselves from criticism, or to reassure another writer. The shifts were not always in the same direction for all writers.

When the TTR for a chunk of text is lower than that individual's mean across all texts, the text presents less lexical diversity and more repetition. Carpenter's findings about speakers suggest that the writer of conversational text might be showing less caution or concern about the reader's reactions. When chunks of text have a higher TTR than the individual's mean, the text presents more lexical diversity and less repetition, which could indicate a greater concern about the reader's reactions. However, those concerns are at the level of the individual: one cannot say that all segments marked with high TTR have the same content across all writers, or even a cohort of writers, across the conference. Instead, it may be more useful to examine where and how high TTR segments are distributed relative to low TTR segments, as departures from the mean suggest that the analyst examine the content, theme, or other feature of text.

For example, the position of high-TTR segments in the corpus, or how they were distributed in general across all the writings, identified a factor that is possibly gender-cued. The Stand Alone conference at the University of North Carolina at Charlotte in the fall 1990 semester contained fifty written entries with at least 150 words, or three fifty-word chunks. Ten of the entries were written by males, thirty-seven by females (three entries were written by mixed-sex dyads, who are not included in the analysis of TTR shift by gender). No single writer started with either a low or high TTR (relative to that individual's mean) and remained at that level. Every writer shifted style as signaled by a shift in the TTR, but they did not all shift in the same direction. Entries typically began with at least two chunks approximating what would eventually be the individual writer's mean for that particular entry, and shifted to either a high or a low level of repetition. Thirty-one entries moved from a high TTR chunk to chunks with low TTR; sixteen entries shifted in the reverse direction.

The pattern of beginning with a high TTR and shifting to a lower may characterize those whom teachers often call "better" writers. The pattern presenting a high level of lexical diversity and a low level of repetition is one typically praised by the educational system and most freshman handbooks. The larger number of unique words, typically multisyllabic and probably Latinate in origin, could be designed to impress the reader, one of whom at some point would be the teacher. The high-to-low TTR pattern may also correlate with gender. Nine of the ten male writers in this conference exhibited the high-to-low pattern, or 90 percent, and twenty-two of the thirty-seven female writers, or just under 60 percent.

TTR identifies segments of a writer's text presenting greater or lesser amounts of diversity. That diversity, as comprised of constellations of lexical and syntactic features, can be used to characterize some features of performance in general by all participants or by specific cohorts in a computer conference. However, TTR is most useful for analyzing the total performance by any single participant. When TTR is run on successive segments by a speaker, the norm for that speaker shows up like a thumbprint, a voiceprint, or a signature. In this study, we have most often used TTR as the signpost to the norm not for a group but for an individual writer. In the study of forensic text, the deviations from the norm identify for the hearers of the testimony a particular stretch of discourse they should investigate more closely in terms of the real-world events being detailed. The deviations from a student's norm in electronic discourse are just as suggestive, for the student will shift, one way or the other. No student created only one frame or style, and wrote only within them. How they shifted is part of their "voiceprint," their discourse signature. Their individual patterns of standard deviations from their mean point toward their "John Hancock" signature.

This signature includes not only the lexical repetition characteristic of the student's mean and deviation, but also a number of syntactic and rhetorical cues. Just as a speaker in a conversation might be habituated to signal a frame or style shift by a cough or change in tone, pitch, intonation, or any other of a variety of linguistic and paralinguistic cues, student writers in the electronic conferences often signaled a style- or frame-shift by their adoption or abandonment of a particular syntactic construction. Within that new frame, the students moved to a different amount of lexical repetition. The interaction between lexicon and syntax, indexed by lexical repetition and charted by TTR analysis of successive chunks of text, signaled changes in the ways students were referring to the language or events in the newspaper stories, to their own memories or opinions, or to each other.

What our corpus archived is a multiparty discussion, which—like the multiparty arguments studied, for example by Charles and Marjorie Goodwin (1992) or the conflict-talk studied by Allan Grimshaw (1990)—was capable of becoming fairly heated. Unlike an argument in conversation, however, the reader/writer can terminate an asynchronous argument at any time without visible rudeness or hostility, simply by stopping the acts of reading or writing.

Guarding the territory

Both high and low TTR segments of the students' writings presented what we are calling "guardedness," but the segments guarded different things. If a writer's high TTR segments usually presented one feature of self-guarding, the low TTR segments usually presented the other. One segment might present the person guarding intellectual property—that is, a self-image in the role of intelligent student who has the ability to interpret difficult or loaded text, and hence has a knowledge-based legitimization to speak with authority on facts, content, issues. The other segment will usually present the person guarding self-image in the role of an enlightened and humane person, interested in others, which affects the amount of personal disclosure, and hence presents an affectively based legitimization to speak with authority on facts, content, issues, and disclosures from other people.

In the example below, from the Transparent conference, "Penny's" autobiographical frame enabled her to establish her credibility to discuss racism in the 1960s from a reported experience, and move to comment on her concerns for the 1990s. In this selection, each full fifty-word segment is preceded by asterisks and the TTR score for the segment. Figure 5.1 shows the TTR shifts in her text.

Since her mean was .8333, with a deviation of .0340, her first and last full segments, at .78 and .88, signal shifts in style. The first segment, the autobiographical frame legitimating her comments to come, presented low diversity and high repetition; the middle segments present the narrative of events told to her and set up a narrative

Figure 5.1. Penny's Thoughts

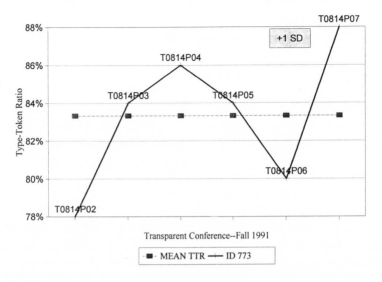

of a parallel event she herself experienced; the last full segment, with the highest diversity and lowest repetition, discloses personal response to the two events juxtaposed.

Penny's Thoughts

*/78/ This is a report about a personal experience. It really isn't personal because my mother experienced it but I have first-hand information.This concerns the sit-ins that began February 1, 1960. My mother was a participant in this historical event in order to help make a change.

At */84/ North Carolina College (now N.C. Central University), students were rallied together by area NAACP leaders and student government leaders.They were instructed to go to a downtown Woolworth and sit at the lunch counter that was only for white customers. They were told to remain calm and when asked by the manager to leave, refuse peacefully.

When */86/ arrested, they were assured that they would be bailed out in a very timely fashion. My mother followed through with the plan and as promised there was no violence. Instead of being herded into a police vehicle, they were escorted to police headquarters on foot.

At headquarters, female and male */84/ students were separated and placed into cells. In approximately eight hours all of the students were released.This experience broadened my perspective on the civil rights movement. It is easy to sit back and say "we are never going to get anywhere," but young college students (like myself) were willing */80/ to make the sacrifice to make a change.

Recently, I was priveleged enough to meet the first Black student to attend this University. Joanna Drake shared the hard times she endured in the early sixties at this university so that people like me can enjoy some privileges she never would */ 88/ have dreamed of. Joanna and her Black roommate shared an entire wing of Shaw hall. In the cafeteria, they ate in a section isolated from everyone else. All of this so that I can live, eat, study and go where I please.

It seems so farfetched or like it happened so long ago,* things have changed but we have a long, long way to go. I can only hope that there will be more [mother's name]'s and Joanna Drakes willing to do their part.

Syntactic cues: Personal pronouns

In students' writings such as Penny's, pronouns have multiple functions. They can, for example, connect text and object; they can indicate the difference between given and new information; their placement, as with the use of *it* in cleft sentences, can signal focus. Their number of occurrences can indicate the degree of self-reference in a text, or suggest how the writer connects to the audience. In the electronic conferences, student writers used personal pronouns to reference both self and events, other persons and states of being; their pronominal usage also indicated time, space, and stance. The students used pronouns to indicate their involvement with three differently authored texts: those written by reporters, those written by other students, and those written by themselves. They used pronouns to refer to themselves, to events within and outside their own immediate experience, and to their audience. What we found in these conferences was an overwhelming use of the pronoun *I*.

Tannen (1989: 76) commented that the repetition of pronouns and discourse markers in conversation "plays a significant role in

Figure 5.2. Personal Pronouns

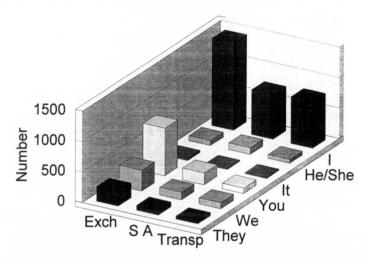

establishing the shared universe of discourse created by conversational interaction in that language." In his study of genres from speech and writing, Biber (1988: 255) noted that the use of the first person pronoun marks a personal focus and involvement with the text. Use of the second person pronoun indicates the writer's high degree of involvement with the addressee. The third person pronouns indicate inexact reference to persons outside the immediate interaction, and may also mark narrative and reported styles. But even though the *I* in the electronic discourse of the computer conferences was self-referential, it did not always have the same force. There was more than one kind of *I* in a student's writing. Even though the *I* referred to that student, it could refer to that student in any of several roles.

In their recent study of *Pronouns and People*, Mühlhäusler and Harré (1990: 92) propose that a pronoun such as *I* has double indexicality; it "indexes whatever is denoted by the speaker's utterance with its spatio-temporal location in relation to the location of the speaker and the moment of his or her utterance (Benveniste 1971). . . . *I* also indexes the utterance with the person who is to be held morally responsible for its illocutionary force and its perlocutionary effects—namely, in English, the speaker." For a number of linguists, beginning with Jespersen's use of the term *shifter* (1922: 123), the pronoun *I* (and also *you*) is a sign that shifts its reference "continually with changes in the speech situation" as noted by Jakobson in 1957 (Jakobson 1990: 386; see p. 69ff. and Silverstein 1976, on distinctions concerning shifters and referential indexicals; see Ochs 1990; Hanks 1992).

For an example of the kinds of roles that the use of first-person pronouns might signify in our multiparty corpus, we looked to the field of debate. It is not unusual for debaters to consider choosing among several different "I"-roles when they must handle controversial issues while establishing credibility or some form of authenticating identification with their audience. Trenholm (1992), for example, listed four different possible projections that a debater might choose (Trenholm 1990: 304), including an *I* to signal personal experience, another to signal authority, a third to signal a kind of audience identification with the speaker, and a fourth which presented the debater's individual method. In the conference writings, we noticed what might be the *I* representing personal experience, and the *I* indicating authority over the text, and possibly a rather humble, ordinary *I* who proffered ideas or notions as opposed to arguments, an *I* with whom readers might identify. The role for *I* depended on the kind of interaction the student writer was framing vis-à-vis the time of the events, actions, or thoughts being presented and the space in which the audience existed.

When we changed the conference interactions by shifting from the Stand Alone to the Transparent conference set-ups, we changed space. What we could not change was time. The events of the Sit-Ins and of the reportage occurred in the 1960s. As visitors to an unknown land, the students faced certain limitations. They could report their perceptions of those events, their reactions, associations, or memories. They could respond or report on their response to the newspaper stories of the past or to the writings of others in the present, and they could affiliate or disaffiliate with the viewpoints presented by any of the texts. What they seldom did, however, was to change from the pervasive *I*, in any of its projections, to the more detached third-person, which characterizes informational text, a more neutral stance, and more abstract argument.

As we reviewed the students' uses of *I*, we found ourselves echoing distinctions drawn thirty years ago by James Moffett in his discussion of "I, You, It" (Moffett 1965), which outlined for composition theory at that time some interconnections between time and stance. In our conferences, the *I*, then or now or somewhere in between, conveyed ideas and reactions to a *you*, the audience at a present time. The *he* was either a reference to the newspaper reporter who wrote text at some time in the far past or to one of the men named in the events reported; *she* was almost always a reference to a classmate who wrote text at some time in the more recent past of now. There were no female by-lines listed for the newspaper stories, so the only way that she could refer to a time other than the weeks of the conference was to some time reported by a student writer as an experience or memory surrounding a female.

As table 5.1 shows, pronouns in the electronic discourse corpus also indexed relations of time, showing how the writers in the conference positioned themselves in time and how they viewed events in relation to that position at the moment of writing.

The student writers preferred to stay in the present and to be involved with their audience of each other, to judge by the way the totals for pronoun tokens arrayed themselves along an axis of then (the sixties) and now (the time of participation in the conferences). The X in the table 5.2 marks the spot where *I*, the writer, surveyed both past and present events and looked to audience:

It *behaves differently*

In her *Theme in English Expository Prose*, Jones (1977; see Martin 1992) noted three ways in which grammar may mark referential

Table 5.1. Pronouns Indexing Relations of Time

I	>then	(in actuality for older students; as projection for most students)
	>now	
you	>now	
he	>then	(reporter, mayor) artifact
she	>now	(female student writer participating in the conference)
it	>now>then	
	>then>now	(anticipatory *it*)
we	>now	
they	>then	

Table 5.2. Student Writers Indexing Time with Pronouns

	they	he		we	you	
			X			
Then	377	255		565	1063	Now

No. of Personal Pronouns in Conferences

prominence. First, one may rearrange word order by placing an object noun phrase at the beginning of the sentence as one way to mark referential prominence: John, I like him. Second, speakers and writers can use special grammatical constructions to mark referential prominence, such as anticipatory-*it* sentences. Third, speakers and writers can use repetition to mark referential prominence, which involves both grammar and reference. All three ways of marking referential prominence involve shifting elements of a sentence in order to foreground or highlight certain information.

The pronoun *it* occurred frequently throughout the corpus of each conference. While *it* was most often used for direct reference to an antecedent in a preceding clause or sentence, *it* was also used to signal prominence, as with the use of the anticipatory-*it* construction. When student writers used the anticipatory *it*, they were indicating what they chose to disclose. At the same time, they were highlighting what they disclosed. The anticipatory-*it* is a grammatical construction that is impersonal. As a syntactic device used to provide discourse signals, the construction provides:

1. A way to provide distance between the writer and the claim made: "It seems to me that . . ." and "It is clear (to me) that . . .";
2. A way to focus on given or shared information in a statement;
3. A way to focus on knowlege the community shares;
4. A discourse signal that the "new" information or argument is yet to come; the reader should "be prepared."

When the students shifted to the new, perhaps controversial, they became more careful. They were more likely to use cataphoric or anticipatory-*it* constructions rather than anaphoric reference. Concomitantly, their TTR scores tended to rise.

Because the situation of open racial confrontation presented in the conference topics was ideologically marked and still controversial, and students—even when on the same campus and in the same classroom during the week—did not always know whose face went with which userid or signature, syntactic features were used with care. Student writers found themselves reacting emotionally and taking ideological stands keyed to the events, to the conventionalized features of sixties journalism, and to contemporary political movements. Most of the address by one writer to another, and thus a powerful norm, was indirect. Students were often able to provide distance between themselves as writers and the controversial topic of the conference by using an impersonal grammatical structure: the anticipatory *it*, termed the extraposed sentence by Otto Jespersen (1922) and others. Two uses of *it* were particularly interesting in terms of how students used the construction to signal different purposes: *it* with *seems* and *it*-clefts.

The use of *it* with *seems* functioned to report the writer's perception rather than the writer's assertion. Stating their perceptions as part of an impersonal construction provided individuals with an additional means with which to distance themselves from a controversial topic. Student writers used the anticipatory -*it* construction 133 times in the Stand Alone conferences, and 120 times in the Transparent conference, most often in constructions like "It is interesting that. . . . sixteen percent (16.67 percent) of those anticipatory-*it* uses occurred with the verbs *seem* or *appear*. *Seem* occurred twenty-nine times in the Stand Alone conference in anticipatory-*it* constructions, and nineteen times in the Transparent conference.

These examples from the Transparent conference illustrate the construction and its use:

1. It seems that there have been different acceptable ways to speak of that race. I remember a time when the preferred label was Afro-American. I also remember the use of black and Negro as acceptable. [Entry T0210]
2. It seems that with the addition of the burning piece of paper in parentheses, that this somehow downgrades the seriousness of the situation and makes it comical in a way. [Refers to "assault with a deadly weapon" in the article.] [Entry T0402]

3. It seems that there are more serious problems in the world for us to argue about than ones between our own people. [Entry T0522]

The following example is the only use of *appear* in the anticipatory-*it* construction:

4. It appears that there were a lot of strong emotions going on in this protest. [Entry T0223]

Biber treats the frequent use of impersonal-*it* as "marking a relatively inexplicit lexical content due to strict time constraints and a non-informational focus" (Biber 1988:226). Both of these characteristics may apply at times to conference writing, but at other times information that is not essentially inexplicit was conveyed through reference to personal experience and individual reaction to journalists.

Cleft constructions, standard in both speaking and writing, provide a way to signal a focus clearly. The *it*-cleft accomplishes the same goal of the anticipatory-*it* construction, if in a different form. The noun phrase to receive the focus is moved toward the beginning of the sentence, although still placed in postverbal position after the be-form inserted as part of the cleft structure:

a. It was the file that the computer mangled.
b. It was the computer that mangled the file.

Cleft constructions do not occur frequently in either speech or writing; they occurred four times in the Stand Alone conferences, six times in the Transparent conference. As Wolfram (1994, 1996) states, however, the infrequency or even obscurity of a particular construction or feature does not remove either its significance or its role in the description of a variety of language.

Gender in the territory

In a detailed discussion of how both grammar and discourse must be examined if variety and variation are to be understood, Ochs (1990: 289) drew on both the grammar of ergative case marking in Samoan and its discourse, or "the norms, preferences, and expectations surrounding its use." She noted that text "structures such as repetition, reformulation, code switching, and various sequential units are also linguistic resources for indexing . . . local contextual dimensions" (293). The dimensions Ochs established are "affective and epistemological dispositions" (295) because "participants' affect and participants' belief and knowledge help to establish their social identity, the social relationship obtaining between them, and the speech act or speech activity they are endeavoring to perform" (296). In at least one instance, gender differences were a crucial factor.

Over the three years of conferences in our corpus, the writers have been two-thirds female, one-third male: this division probably characterizes undergraduate enrollment in English courses, at least in the southeast. Neither the corpus nor the writers can be seen as representative of any global norms; they are a stratified sample of students. However, we are not attempting to characterize all writers of asynchronous, extemporaneous electronic discourse, at least not immediately. Limited by the fact that we know of no other comparable corpus of interactive conference writers by novices in the virtual scriptorium, we cannot perform external comparisons, or conduct external reconstruction. Instead, we are limited to looking at different aspects of the corpus over its time span of three years.

Even within those constraints, however, some gender differences showed themselves rather quickly. Titles, for example, presented some gender-cued characteristics. TTR signaled shifts of discourse, which, in a larger sense, may also be seen as gender-based. We found that we could characterize some few norms for asynchronous electronic conference writing across all the writers in the corpus; very quickly, however, we saw a subset of norms for female writers that differed from the subset for male writers in predictable ways.

It would be incorrect, we think, to establish one or the other gender as the unmarked, hence expected, norm and see the other as divergent, based solely on plurality. For computer-supported writing, this is not a trivial issue, since face-to-face and oral paralinguistic cues for gender are absent. And, though userids were clearly present on the screen, provided by the software, unless students signed their name, used their name in their posting title, or referred to themselves in a way that disambiguated their gender, the only way for gender cues to surface was in written, semianonymous text. (And, we hasten to add, names alone are not sufficient gender cues in the south, and possibly elsewhere: "Chris," "Lee," "Beverly,"and other names as well as nicknames are borne by both males and females.) We began, then, by looking at whether norms and plurality coincided, since we could imagine situations in which the norm for a community was keyed to the plurality of speakers, if and as that plurality were also seen as dominant, privileged, or most powerful.

Because there were more females than males in our classes, and a minimum number of writings was specified, the total number of writings alone did not a norm establish. Our data do not substantiate a claim that males might volunteer more frequently than females. There were more writings by females than by males, just in terms of the total number of all writings. The percentages of females who wrote more than the minimum number of entries, compared to all females, was only slightly larger, however, than the percentages of males compared to all males. And, again looking at comparative percentages, the number of writings by women that met our conditions for TTR analysis were roughly equivalent, compared to all women's writings, to the number of males. Our data did not substantiate a claim that identifies either sex as likely to write more text, any more than it could substantiate a claim that either sex was likely to write more frequently.

Instead, we propose that, within the general set of norms for all writers in the conference, there were subsets of norms that are gender-marked, and were seen as gender-marked by readers of the writing. What then happens, of course, is that one of those sets of gender-cued norms may be "privileged" by social factors affecting reader expectations. In Myers-Scotton's careful discussion of social motivations underlying code switching, she noted that her analysis, particularly that of code switching as a negotiation of identity, rested on the premise that "speakers and addressees know (as part of their communicative competence) that choice of one linguistic variety rather than another expresses social import" (1993b: 151). This implies, she added, that "speakers have some sense of 'script' or 'schema' for how interactions are to be conducted in an unmarked way" (152). That script or schema, that set of expected conventions, is specific to the community the speakers are in. And part of that set of conventions would seem to be gender-cued. For us, analyzing the writing in multiparty discourse in asynchronous computer conferencing, that interactive conference discourse becomes the temporary community. We hold that gender is a part of the conventions within this community, gender not as sex alone, but as part of the writer's role as well.

For example, male writers shifted tense to indicate they were moving into an act of challenge; they more often presented challenge, while female writers more often presented elaborated explanation of claims. Here, see the distinctions between report-talk and rapport-talk, for males and females, as elaborated by Tannen (1990: 73ff. see notes pp. 302–3). Male writers were more likely to present both a high and a low TTR chunk, with the low-TTR chunk—high variety, low repetition—immediately preceding the high one. Female writers, on the other hand, often began with their mean, moved to a passage with high repetition, and then shifted to greater lexical diversity.

In other words, the male writers moved from claiming authority keyed to text and action to one that opened the possibility for affiliation through empathy or personal disclosure—if they so chose—while female writers typically began with affiliation and moved to authority based on text and past action. When and how writers shift to their high- or low-TTR segments was, then, gender-marked as well. Regardless of whether they began with a high- or a low-TTR chunk, males typically started off immediately with a chunk so marked, and then faded back to their mean, switching one to two chunks later to the reverse marking. Females, on the other hand, were as likely to begin with one or more chunks at their mean before moving to their peaks and dips of lexical diversity as they were to start with a marked chunk.

A writing whose first chunk was marked for either high or low TTR was, in effect, moving immediately into establishing common ground with the audience and the authority of the writer either through demonstrating authority over the text in the prompt or by affective affiliation. When we considered that over half the female writings marked for TTR began with the mean and then moved most frequently into a passage marked for high repetition and low diversity, we saw that the females presented a greater range of variation and that they often moved to affiliative and affective claims before moving to the high diversity TTR-passage. These high diversity, low repetition chunks were more filled with nominals: this "informational" feature is characteristic of scientific discourse (Biber

1988; see Witte and Cherry 1986). It looks weighty; it looks serious. Just as males and females often talk at what Tannen calls cross-purposes (Tannen 1990:42ff.), they may be writing there as well.

Brent's territorial moves

Writers in the physical context and topical territories of the electronic conferences busily shifted styles within a single stretch of writing, directed to an audience they could not see, but that they felt to be present because of the multiple postings possible in asynchronous conferencing. Such style shifts, like code shifts, had multiple functions. Writers who wrote postings that were marked by both high or low TTR shifts received in general more attention in the form of direct replies, either to the writing or to the writer. Indirect referentiality was also important: showing sentence-level reference throughout one conference topic, figure 5.3 shows how often every sentence had reference beyond the writer's spontaneous overflow of powerful feelings evoked by the hot issues in the newspaper stories of the sit-ins.

Brent never directly challenged another writer in the conference. He preferred to challenge the newspaper texts and to establish his credibility with his audience by resonating themes or topics they had mentioned in their writings. Here Brent's idiolect served the

Figure 5.3. Four–way Reference in Topic 3

1 Link to text—prompt **79**	2 Link to self-writing **48**
4 No link **11**	3 Link to other writing **5**

community within the conference by knitting together their discussions. Typical of his multilayered, polyphonic writing is the excerpt below, the eleventh writing in Stand Alone's topic 3. Figure 5.4, which follows his writing, displays in a linear mode the ways he resonated previous student writings in the first sentence of his opening chunk as he both directly addressed the newspaper story that headed the Topic, and inserted his own opinions.

In this article, Roy Covington refers to "mass requests for service" by groups of 3 to 40 black students. Had they been white, it is doubtful that this number of customers would have been noteworthy. "Mass" is an overstatement. Unintentional or not, Covington's piece implies that a tone of underlying menace—black menace—was about to make its way into the "heart of downtown" Charlotte. Lock up the women!

Military imagery is found throughout the article. Despite the denials of Charles Jones, Covington asserts that Mr. Jones is "clearly one of the field generals." By noting Jones' denials of what Covington deems to be obvious truth, the reporter plants a prejudicial seed in the readers' minds. Can the readers be sure of the truthfulness of anything that Jones or his followers say in the rest of the article?

We are told that one group "takes up its positions" at a lunch counter. With such a band of outsiders invading the eating places, this piece almost seems like a call to arms. I am surprised that there is no reference to patrols or regiments of students.

The article notes "darkened counters" resulted from the students' appearance and the subsequent suspension of food service. I wonder about the use of darkened. Were counters darkened by the removal of artificial light at midday, or by the color of the demonstrators' skin?

When the students were turned away at one counter, they would go to another "in rapid succession." When considered within the context of the entire piece, this characterization paints a picture of a well-drilled group of protestors eager to undermine traditions. Even the infamous House Committee on UnAmerican Activities is referred to, and Charles Jones is again referred to. If passions had not yet been aroused, then surely this would work.

> A return to normalcy is seen at the end of the article. Under the watchful eye of the police, the unpredictable protestors become "visitors," and order is restored. "There were no incidents."

Brent's textual voice, like his speaking voice, seemed smooth, even soft, at first. Readers, like hearers, were lulled by its tone into an argument that moved them into new territory and suddenly snapped shut behind them.

Figure 5.4. First Sentence by Brent

Note: X = indirect Words/Phrases	Issues	Writings									
		1	2	3	4	5	6	7	8	9	10
In this article	Previous writers using "this"	▓	▓			▓	▓	▓			
	Previous writers summarizing ...	▓	▓	▓	▓	▓	▓	▓			
	Direct exchange 9 agrees with 1	▓			<				▓	<	
Roy Covington	Author of original story with by-line										
refers to "mass requests for service"	College students	▓									
	Negro college students	▓			▓	▓					
	Requests for service		▓		X	X	X	▓			
	Mass +count/+threat				X		X		X		
by groups of 3 to 40 black students	Issue of "mass" begins				▓						

6:// Taking a stance: Text, self, and other

The term *idiolect* describes the language of an individual speaker—that is, the range of preferred or habitual features that mark an individual's way of speaking. These features are viewed as idiomatic rather than systematic as they reflect individual choices made in the context of social influence. Bloomfield noted that close observation would show that "no two persons . . . spoke exactly alike." Although a newcomer into a community may speak so much like us that his speech may not cause "the slightest difficulty in communication," he added, but yet the speech may be "strikingly noticeable on account of inessential differences, such as accent and idiom (1933: 45).

Lehmann (1962: 143) stated that the idiolect, the language of a single speaker, consists of "multistrata units" related to a speaker's change in "his place of living, his social status, his relations to his associates, his occupation," factors that may force the speaker to "introduce changes in his language."

Labov (1969: 759) noted that "the grammar of the speech comunity is more regular and systematic than the behavior of any one individual. . . . Unless the individual speech pattern is studied within the over-all system of the community, it will appear as a mosaic of unaccountable and sporadic variation."

In electronic conference discourse, variation is presented by written text composed by individual writers, each drawing on idiolectal preferences from their full repertoire of oral and written discourse.

Aspects of modality

In the absence of being able to see each other face to face, and without a history of prior acquaintance with each other, individuals writing in electronic conferences manipulate language in some interesting ways in order to express themselves. For example, they can draw on their language's system of *modality*, a complex category frequently explained as "the grammaticalization of speakers' (subjective) attitudes and opinions" (Palmer 1986:16). A sentence such as "Henry can open the window now" could present what is called epistemic modality: Henry is capable of opening the window. However, that sentence could also be an indirect command conferring obligation upon Henry, or it might reflect the obligation or necessity under which Henry labors; in that case, we would distinguish different types of modality to refer to which sense—possibility, probability, necessity, or obligation—is being suggested.

Language systems have a variety of ways their users can employ in order to distinguish such shades of meaning such as the degree to which a speaker/writer might convey assertion or evidentiality. In the electronic conferences, the students were writing extemporaneous responses to newspaper texts about race and conflict, as well as to each others' responses. Looking at some aspects of modality—even though modality is defined and studied from different perspectives—should illuminate ways the students decided how assertive they might want to be in terms of writing about a hot topic, knowing that their peers and their teachers would read what they had to say. Looking at features of modality—such as the presence of modal verbs in particular collocations—may ultimately contribute to understanding why many react to electronic discourse as if it were spoken conversation, when its form is actually written text.

Modality comes with the territory of saying or writing something. Different languages draw on different morphological, syntactic, and lexical structures in order to mark it: Palmer notes that the marking can be by modal verbs, by mood (signaled in many languages by inflectional affixes), by particles, and by clitics (1986: 33). It is reasonable to expect that individual students writing in any of the electronic conferences would have individual ways of drawing on and marking modality within written English text to express what they wanted to mean in their writing and possibly to signal how they felt or what they thought about what they were writing. What is interesting—and an implication for future research on electronically composed text—is how different kinds of modality were used.

While we begin with a review of definitions of modality, our emphasis is not on its theoretical underpinnings, nor can we say that extemporaneous composition on keyboards will "change" features of modality in either written or spoken English. Instead, what we are looking at is how students as a group and students as individuals selected different features of English to indicate their attitudes and opinions, while in the general situation of keyboard composition. Then we present a comparison of their use across two specific situations, the Stand Alone and the Transparent constructs. We look first at their frequencies for use of modal verbs, then at the interaction of modals with downtoners, amplifiers, and similar lexical items, which shade the meaning of the verb. Next we look at their use of modals and downtoners in co-occurence with negation, and at when these features correlated with students' choices of public and private verbs. Finally, we describe how modality functioned as part of the students' general shifts in style (keyed to lexical variety) within successive fifty-word chunks of student writings, and look closely at one writing by an individual student.

We are not claiming that the students did not already have and use particular constellations of each of these features, which may make up modality in either their speaking or their writing outside of the conference—for of course, they did. Modality, and the ways one marks it, are part of the individual language repertoires that the students brought to the conference. Instead, we want to demonstrate first, how individual students presented and sustained markers of modality as part of their choices to express themselves. And second, we want to show how the group of students writing in one kind of conference displayed modality slightly differently as a whole from those writing in another kind of conference. The social situation of two different constructs for interactive participation, in other words, may have presented the group having fewer ties to each other with a greater impetus for certain patterns of expression.

Modality: A range of definitions

Depending on their primary emphasis on either formalist or functionalist analyses of language (Schiffrin 1994: 27ff.), scholars present different ways to analyze modality, involving both grammatical and semantic aspects. Without going too far astray from our main focus—which is to describe and analyze how students used modal verbs, and the ways these forms interacted or co-occurred with other features, in order to invoke shades of meaning—it will be helpful to review how different scholars study modality.

For example, Stubbs, drawing on work by Chafe, notes that all languages have *evidentials,* which are ways for their speakers/ writers to use some feature of modality to encode "the degree of reliability the person attributes to a proposition and the source of the knowledge (for example, direct personal experience, hearsay, inference)" (Stubbs 1996: 147; see Chafe and Nichols 1986). Speakers and writers, according to Stubbs, present evidentiality in different ways (see 200–02; 63–64). One could say that speakers more often present personal opinion than academic writers, who present text-cued information. In the electronic conferences, student writers varied between these two ways of presenting evidentiality. If their writings were shorter than about seventy-five words (roughly the length of the portion of screen visible to the writer beginning to write a reply to a text on the screen, or ten lines of seventy-one spaces each), the student either presented personal opinion or text-cued information. If their writings were 150 words or longer, the students usually presented both.

Palmer's 1986 study, *Mood and Modality,* reminds us that different languages draw on different features of their systems in order to present modality, which involves grammatical marking, usually but not always associated with the verbal system. However, as Palmer notes, when we look at modality as a general phenomenon across languages it "does not relate semantically to the verb alone or primarily, but to the whole sentence" (Palmer 1986:2). And, as Palmer adds (p. 14), a distinction can be made between the speaker's attitude or opinion and the way the speaker presents the proposition of the sentence in which that attitude or opinion is expressed. The distinction between proposition and modality is thus, claims Palmer, "very close to that of locutionary act and illocutionary act" in that the first says and the second does. Hence modality is tied into the ways we classify sentence types, and types of speech acts. A wider definition of modality, in reference to nonpropositional elements of a sentence, could include tense, aspect, question, negation, and mood, though different theoreticians assign different features to the category of modality.

Palmer's review of distinctions between epistemic and root, or deontic, modality is useful: epistemic modality refers to a modal system that involves "the notions of possibility and necessity . . . [and] indicates the degree of commitment by the speaker to what he says" (p. 51). Root modality refers to the ways a sense of obligation is signaled. In many instances, the same forms, such as modal verbs, express both modalities: may and must can express the epistemic judgment "Lee may/must be in Chicago", as well as the root directive "Lee must come tomorrow." When we look at the impact of different modal verbs, and more specifically at the forms students chose from the modal system, we draw on the kinds of formal distinctions from philosophical semantics as explained by Palmer.

Bybee, Perkins, and Pagliuca (1994) examine the most commonly occurring grammatical categories across languages, looking at the notion "that formally identifiable morphemes in the languages of the world have certain semantic properties and are drawn from certain areas of semantic space" (37). Their work draws on a basic insight from Bybee 1985: "deontic or agent-oriented modalities usually have periphrastic expression while subordinating and epistemic moods are usually inflectional" (xv). When we look at how specific modal verbs co-occur with qualifiers and public and private verbs, we find their four categories for modality to be helpful:

- *agent-oriented*, which is often called deontic, uses markers of modality to report (177), "internal/external conditions on an agent with respect to the completion of the action expressed in the main predicate" (which in some studies would not be considered modality): these include the expression of desires, obligations, abilities, and intentions;
- *speaker-oriented* markers of modality refer, in the case of verbs and modal verbs, to "those with which the speaker performs an act" (301). Their use allows the speaker to impose conditions on the person being addressed, and the grammatical terms used by Bybee, Perkins, and Pagliuca for such acts include the imperative, prohibitive, optative, hortative, admonitive, and permissive (179);

- *epistemic* markers "express the degree of assertion of the speaker" (301) in that "markers of epistemic modality indicate something less than a total commitment by the speaker to the truth of the proposition" (179);
- *subordinating* markers of modality are "those that occur regularly in certain types of subordinate clauses" and are often (180) the same forms that express speaker-oriented and epistemic modalities).

Bybee, Perkins, and Pagliuca expand Palmer's definition and adapt it to their examination of how modality is grammaticized over time, for which they seek "statistical support for the hypothesis that formal change proceeds in parallel with semantic change in grammaticization" (279). Halliday (1994), on the other hand, does something very different. Halliday's *Introduction to Functional Grammar* (1994) focuses on the interplay of usage, system, and function: that is, how the textual, ideational, and interpersonal meanings of language function within the total linguistic system, from the viewpoint of systemic theory as a series of networks of choices, and with the goal of analyzing a spoken or written text. Analysis, for Halliday, enables us to "show how, and why, the text means what it does" and to move to evaluating "why the text is, or is not, an effective text for its own purposes" (1994:xv). For Halliday, modality "refers to the area of meaning that lies between yes and no" (356), since "speakers have indefinitely many ways of expressing their opinions—or rather, perhaps, of dissumulating the fact that they *are* expressing their own opinions"(353).

Working from the opposition between assertion and negation (what he calls positive and negative polarity), Halliday distinguishes degrees of probability and of usuality as presented either for the proposition, or statements, and questions, or the proposal, offers, and commands, noting that both probability and usuality can be expressed for either propositions or proposals by "a finite modal operator in the verbal group [should, will] . . . a modal Adjunct [for example, 'probably' 'always'] . . . or both together" (1994:89).

Although we are not working specifically within Halliday's notion of polarity, we use functionalist insights when we look at how different features cluster within what we are calling narrachunks and then examine these features as they characterize each writer's habits of expressing or dissimulating their opinions. Following Schiffrin (1994), we believe that insights from formalist and functionalist scholarship can help to characterize discourse in general and electronic discourse in particular.

It is possible, says Schiffrin in *Approaches to Discourse* (1994), to look both at form and function, and at the interactions between context and use, and text and context. To do that, she expands the formalist notion that discourse is language above the sentence beyond looking at hierarchies of successively larger units to look instead at the organization and structure of discourse as "emergent" within a framework that posits discourse as utterances. She begins by adopting Lyons's distinction between text sentences ("context-dependent utterance-signals") and system sentences ("well-formed strings generated by the grammar" (27; citations to Lyons 1977:385, 387, 622) in order to ground her claims that discourse is keyed to utterance as opposed to sentence in the sense that "discourse arises not as a collection of decontextualized units of language structure, but as a collection of inherently contextualized units of language use" (39).

If, says Schiffrin, we assume that text is the linguistic content in the sense of propositional meanings, and context is the environment, "a world filled with people producing utterances" (363), then "describing the text/context relationship may require empirical analyses of different aspects of texts, different aspects of contexts . . . and the ways they are bound to one another" (385). We follow Schiffrin's lead and Biber's example by examining first, occurrences of public, private, and suasive verbs, then at how and when these verbs co-occur with modals and qualifiers in differently situated conferences within our corpus.

The individual and the text

How and when did the student writers qualify the force of their assertions, claims, challenges, and indicate to the reader something about the degree of the writer's confidence relating to a particular assertion? The presentation of clusterings of modal verbs in co-occurrence with public or private verbs, qualifiers, and lexical variation can be taken as representing solidarity, deference, involvement, or independence as students presented an identity constructed through text, in response to text or to what they perceived as a type of text. For example, some of the students chose self-disclosure as their sole, or primary, or predominant source of evidence, self-authorization, and legitimatization. It would be reasonable to expect them to use different grammatical features to express their meaning from those who chose to offer authorization of their "voice" from texts or from a construct of assumptions about shared and given cultural knowledge. A number of students mixed their text types. We can see this not only in the amount of variation presented in each text-type, but also in the kinds of modal verbs and qualifiers that co-occurred in the different narrachunks or segments of their written discourse.

Looking at individual features and then at clusters of kinds of verbs, modal verbs, and qualifiers lets us examine the individual's preferences for creating electronic discourse, or their idiolects. To a certain extent we can see that a corpus of conference e-discourse, because of its interactive nature, is an anthology of individuals each presenting their own idiolects as opposed to a collaborative text designed to present a single voice.

Verb classes

Following Biber (1988) we reviewed four verb classes that have specific functions. (These verb classes are discussed extensively in *A Comprehensive Grammar of Contemporary English* by Quirk, Greenbaum, Leech, and Svartvik 1985; see Greenbaum and Quirk 1990.) *Public* verbs, Biber reminds us, involve "actions that can be publicly observed," including speech act/performative verbs like *say* and *explain*. *Private* verbs like *think* and *know* are "verbs of cognition" that refer to mental activities. *Suasive* verbs "imply intentions to bring about some change in the future." *Seem/Appear*, verbs of perception, "mark evidentiality with respect to the reasoning process . . . and they represent another strategy used for academic hedging"(Biber 1988:242). Each of these classes of verbs may be drawn upon by the speaker/writer as a way to shade or specify particular meanings of utterances.

Table 6.1. Frequency for Six Private Verbs

Verb	Frequency	Percent
think	591	40.04
feel	246	16.67
see	192	13.01
know	171	11.59
find	156	10.57
understand	120	8.13
Totals	1,476	100.01

Note: Because the numbers are rounded, the total does not equal 100 percent.

In order to see how the student writers as a whole indicated thoughts as opposed to feelings, we checked the lists of verbs that Biber used for his study. Private verbs appeared more frequently than either of the other classes. Thirty-four private verbs were used 2,311 times. Six private verbs occurred more than 100 times in the conferences, for a total of 1,476 uses, with the verb *think* accounting for slightly more than one-fourth of the uses of private verbs.

There were twenty-three public verbs, used 901 times. Only three of the twenty-three public verbs occurred more than 100 times, and these accounted for 594, or nearly two-thirds, of all uses.

Suasive verbs, nineteen in all, accounted for 294 uses. Only one suasive verb, *agree*, was used more than 100 times in the three electronic conferences. *Agree* is also a public verb.

Table 6.2. Frequency of Three Public Verbs

Verb	Frequency	Percent
say	333	56.06
agree	150	25.25
write	111	18.69
Totals	594	100.00

Table 6.3. Frequency of Four Suasive Verbs

Verb	Frequency	Percent
agree	150	60.24
ask	52	20.88
suggest	26	10.44
decide	21	8.43
Totals	249	99.99

Note: Because the numbers are rounded, the total does not equal 100 percent.

The verbs of perception *seem* and *appear* occurred 406 times in the electronic conferences. The verb *seem* was used 386 times, accounting for 90.6 percent of the verbs in this group. *Appear* occurred thirty-eight times (9.4 percent). Almost two-thirds of the uses of *seem* (62.3 percent) occurred in the anticipatory-*it* constructions.

Clearly, the private verbs were the major class of verbs represented in the electronic conferences. As students were writing to share information and opinions about a culturally sensitive and socially controversial topic, and to present their interpretation of language use at the time of the Sit-Ins, the students frequently used the class of verbs that indicates involvement with an audience.

Why were they using private verbs? They were visiting another time; they could not really interact with the events of thirty years earlier. Private verbs reported their perceptions of long ago events to other participants in the here and now in a way that allowed the other participants to share their perceptions. In that sense the use of private verbs was a politeness strategy and an invitation to other participants to share their own perceptions.

Table 6.4. Frequency of *Seem* and *Appear*

Verb	Frequency	Percent
appear	38	9
seem	368	91
Totals	406	100

Seventy-six percent of the uses of *know* (in any tense) appeared in the chunks for which TTR-analysis indicated a shift in frame or register signaled by high diversity/low repetition, and forty percent of the uses of *think*. Women were proportionately more likely to use each of these specific verbs, usually in "I think/know that...." clauses; men stated their claims without the introductory phrase of thinking or knowing. It may be that the more frequent appearance of each of these verbs in the high TTR chunks suggests gender-cued acts of planning, staging, framing, or of allusion and quotation. However, we temper that suggestion with a good deal of caution; *think* and *know* (as with other private verbs) appeared almost invariably in complementary distribution for any individual writer. That is, *think* did not show up in a chunk where *know* appeared, and vice versa. The appearance of each verb signaled some sort of frame-shift, or the move to a different text type, and the verb's appearance was usually in co-occurence with other features.

For example, students writing entries of 150 words or longer, seldom used *feel* or single-word synonyms for this verb; instead, they "showed" the reader how they felt with adjectives and phrases. *Feel* (or its synonyms) almost always occurred in complementary distribution with verbs of thinking, knowing, or remembering. Modals also occurred for individual writers in complementary distribution with each other, and with verbs of thinking, knowing, or feeling. Modals characterized neither high TTR (high diversity) or low TTR (low diversity) passages. Instead, they were used as bridges between or as staging for passages marked by diversity at either end. They were a back-up, wait-and-see, signal of movement to come.

We examined how students used modal verbs in the Stand Alone and Transparent conferences, looking first at uses by the group of students and then at individual usage. Some general statements can be made about the co-occurence of modals with different types of verbs:

Can: was only once used with *think, know,* or *believe*; instead, it co-occurred with single verbs of perception, action, or being, and always indicated potential, possibility, or intent. In negated forms, *can't/cannot* occurred primarily with single verbs of perception and memory.

Could: was never used with *think/know*; instead, *could* co-occurred with single verbs of action, perception, or state of being.

Should: was used less by TTR writers, who were generally less prescriptive for themselves or others; instead, *should* co-occurred with states of being.

Will: was used invariably to mark intent-for-future when self-referring, and marked futurity if referring to anything else.

Would: never co-occurred with *think/know* or even with *feel*; marked either action or state of being. When it marked states of being and was self-referring to the writer, it included a sense of futurity as well as of purpose.

While social cues are present in electronic discourse, just as they can be in any written text, they are certainly reduced below the level found in face-to-face or even voice-to-voice conversation. However, since e-conferences (and probably e-mail and e-messages) can be said to run on the individual's horsepower, individuals may feel obliged or constrained to present overt markers of stance and conviction, so that the reader has the sense of responding to a person, not a screen.

Contexts and modal verbs

A closer look at modal verbs and their immediately preceding contexts may suggest how an individual's selections of features suggesting modality might reflect emulation at the level of what Scollon and Scollon describe as dimensions of interpretive frames within the discourse system (1995:168–71, 232–33). Here, Scollon and Scollon look at a series of dimensions used by Tannen 1990 to analyze intergender discourse, noting that these are "dimensions along which men and women tend to form different interpretive frames" (232). These dimensions, particularly when compared with the kinds of dimensions established by Biber for analyzing the continuum from speech to writing, can be quite suggestive. For example, Scollon and Scollon look at the dimension of relationship—information, noting that "the use of deductive or inductive strategies for the introduction of topics was related to the question of whether relationship or informational functions of language predominated" (234). In many instances, women are perceived to focus more on relationships than men, who tend to focus more on information.

In the electronic conferences, we noted that students created at least two distinct text-types, often mixing them in the same entry. The different segments or narrachunks of entries differed in their amount of lexical repetition; they differed as well in their presentation of different grammatical features. Were these keyed in any way to issues of gender, or solidarity, or status? Looking at grammatical features within the contextualized utterances of electronic discourse might be a way to identify the presence or absence of salient differences or tendencies keyed to such constructs. It might also be a way to begin to discern when variation and repetition was keyed to a possible process of group or cohort socialization and when to the individual's own idiolectal preferences.

We began by looking in each of the two conferences, since they could be said to present different social situations in terms of perceived audience, at how writers combined modals with a preceding construct of *I/We* (self and self plus a construct of group, represented by pronouns) and with a construct of *Other* (not me, not my group, represented by third-person pronouns, *there*-constructions, or noun phrases). How confident is the writer, represented by "I," about asserting on behalf of self or self-and-we or on behalf of others? That raises the issue of when and how does a modal indicate deference or solidarity in electronic discourse. Most verbal constructions with modal verbs other than "can" were not qualified. Following Palmer's distinctions between possibility, probability and obligation (1990:34–37, 58–59) we have distinguished between *can, can't,* and *cannot.*

In the Transparent conference, the writers assert, with varying degrees of confidence, the epistemic for the self and the immediate group, with *can, cannot,* and *can't* do, be, or perceive, but ascribe or project obligation on the Other with *may, must, would, should,* and *could.* In the Stand Alone conference, the writer/our-group construct was less frequently signaled by the combination of clausal subject plus modal verb (and main verb). We found no significant difference, as measured by chi-square tests, between the two conferences when tabulated for all modals against all modals-SA, by *mustwe*-T as opposed to *mustwe*-SA or by the assignment of modals to *it/they* as opposed to *I/we* tokens for either conference. Writers in the two conferences patterned alike in terms of confidence of assertion, as measured by frequency of occurrence for *I/we* uses of

Table 6.5. Self and Other

	Transparent I/We	Stand Alone I/We	Transparent Other	Stand Alone Other
must	33	22	67	78
should	12	13	71	83
would	24	21	69	76
could	14	16	79	68
may	15	10	85	90
can	43	46	45	38
can't	67	70	29	30
cannot	79	67	7	33

Numbers indicate percentages of occurrence.

modals and the assignment of modals to Others, whether the Other was represented by the generic (*it/they*) or by specified noun phrases.

Next, we examined the most frequent verbs of thinking (as suggesting the informational) and feeling (as suggesting dimension of involvement or of potential relationships), in order to see how these verbs co-occured with modals and qualifiers. Did writers confidently assert what they did know as opposed to what they didn't? Did they assert what they knew, but with little confidence? In order to assess the possible impact of the expansion of audience via the Transparent conference, we looked at what these collocations might mean in terms of their degree of politeness to others. By qualifiers, we mean adverbs such as "always, usually, sometimes," adjuncts such as "only, just," and markers of negation, such as "no, not, never": these are often called hedges, downtoners, emphatics, and intensifiers (see Biber 1988:240–41).

The student writers in both conferences presented high confidence in asserting and ascribing *I/we* thinking and believing in terms both of frequency of main verb and the minimal number of qualifiers. They had slightly less confidence in their acts of finding (used in the sense of a cognitive discovery following an act of evaluation) and knowing. They indicated some need to qualify acts of remembering, agreeing, or liking, even though presenting high confidence in terms of the frequency for asserting or ascribing these acts on behalf of self and group.

Table 6.6. Co-Occurence of Verbs of Thinking and Feeling with Modals and Qualifiers, Transparent Conference

Main Verb	Tokens	I	We	Qualified by Adverb or Modal		Negated Forms (+/- Modal)	
	N	N	N	%	N	%	N	%
believe	28	18	2	71	4	14	5	18
feel	53	34	0	64	5	9	0	
think	99	78	1	80	1	1	14	14
find	36	24	1	69	9	25	0	
know	47	24	2	55	3	6	8	17
remember	14	12	0	85	4	29	1	7
agree	43	40	3	100	12	28	5	12
like	24	21	1	92	9	38	1	4
hate	0							

Table 6.7. Co-Occurence of Verbs of Thinking and Feeling with Modals and Qualifiers, Stand Alone Conference

Main Verb	Tokens	I	We	Qualified by Adverb or Modal		Negated Forms (+/- Modal)	
	N	N	N	%	N	%	N	%
believe	24	12	0	50				
feel	17	10	0	59	2	11	0	
think	64	47	0	73	0		4	8
find	14	13	0	92	2	14	0	
know	25	9	0	36	2	8	2	8
remember	10	5	0	50	0		4	40
agree	16	14	2	100	2	13	0	
like	14	8	1	64	8	47	3	21
hate	6	5	0	83	2	33	0	

No significant difference highlights the ways student writers as a group drew on different features of modality for either the Stand Alone or Transparent conferences. Instead, we think that individuals shaded their meaning according to whether they were presenting self-legitimatization from personal memory and experience or from text. Their use of modals and qualifiers was dependent on the main verb they selected from their repertoire, according to their own habitual preferences for using verbs of perception, memory, and proclamation within a particular text type. Certain verbs, usually private verbs, were apparently felt by their users to require some sort of polite qualification, deference, or demurral within a multiparty interactive electronic discourse, in order to maintain solidarity (see Stubbs 1996:202). What we cannot, of course, establish is the degree of sincerity writers actually felt; we can only discuss the degree of sincerity they chose to present under such constraints.

What may be of greater import is to look at the impact a particular modal verb, qualifier, or main verb had within an individual writing, or at how any one individual writer habitually chose certain collocations, as part of that writer's idiolect. Table 6.8 shows the kinds of complementary distribution of modals, public, and private verbs, and qualifiers (negation, intensifiers, downtoners, and emphatics) that student writers in the Transparent conference employed. This pattern of complementary distribution shows up in separate segments or narrachunks whether analyzed by type-token ratio into successive fifty-word chunks or by the analysis of narrative elements (see appendix to chapter 4). Table 6.8 shows selected writers from the forty-nine entries in topic 2 of the Transparent conference; the table analyzing all topic 2 entries of more than 150 words is appended to this chapter.

The correlation between the distribution of features and the type-token ratio is both intricate and apparent: for example, the writer of entry 217 used *think* in segments with low TTR, and *feel, know* and *say* in chunks with high TTR. For this writer, the presence or absence of modal verbs or negation has no correlation with shifts between parts of a narrative or between text types, either of which is signaled by changes in TTR. However, the appearance of modals and the use of the intensifier "just" signals the shifts for the writer of entry 208, while negation marks the higher segments for entry 207. The patterning of features is very much an individual matter.

A change in audience

When examined for frequency at the group level, the clusterings of public and private verbs, modal verbs, and qualifiers seemed to pattern alike for writers in both the Stand Alone and Transparent

Table 6.8. Modals, Public, and Private, Verbs, Qualifiers, and Negation, Transparent Entries 202, 207, 208, 217, 229

Entry Number	Campus	Chunk 1	Chunk 2	Chunk 3	Chunk 4	Chunk 5	Chunk 6
202	UNCC Sec. 2	70 really private: find	84 private: believe	74	82 only public: suggest	80 Public: suggest could be 3	86 a lot
207	UNCC Sec. 1	70 private: felt private: remember	90 only private: find private: hope could relate? 3	86 really can't work? 3	~		
208	UNCC Sec. 1	78 private: meant	86 just	80 only private: noticed	84 just only IF	~ public: explained private: know/–neg	

continued on next page

Table 6.8. (continued)

Entry Number	Campus	Chunk 1	Chunk 2	Chunk 3	Chunk 4	Chunk 5	Chunk 6
217	UNCG	76	84	74	90	82	~
			really	IF	really		private: think
		private: think-neg	private: feel	Private: think	public: say		
		private: think-neg	private: know	private: think	private: know		
		private: thought	private: understand-neg		*cannot say*		
229	UNCC Sec. 1	68	80	78	82	76	~
		IF		just			private: think
			private: know	private: think-neg	private: think-neg	private: feel	*could have been 3*
			private: mean			private: think	*could have shown 3*
						can find out	

Notes:

numbers = TTR for that segment

~ = Indicates a segment that had fewer than fifty words (but did have twenty-five or more words); did not calculate TTR for these segments

shading = A segment with negation

conferences. However, when the patterns of complementary distribution for features in individual entries in each conference were reviewed more closely, different, even idiosyncratic patternings emerged. It is not frequency of forms alone that describes patterning—that is, whether students in one conference presented more features than another—but by the ways the features were distributed across segments, and how the writer chose to use them in segments showing high or low amounts of lexical repetition. Where the writings for the Transparent conference present reasonably transparent patternings for complementary distribution, those for the Stand Alone conference are a bit more subtle. But they are there; see table 6.9.

For example, in two adjoining chunks, if chunk 1 presents private verb and so does chunk 2, and there is a sizable (more than one standard deviation) TTR shift between the chunks, then the private verb in the first chunk will carry +negation, and in the second chunk will omit negation. Or the verb will be in the first person for chunk 1 and in the 3rd person for chunk 2, or it will be inflected for present tense in one segment, and shift to past tense in the next. If there is not a sizable TTR shift between those chunks, then those two chunks will either be part of the same narrative (where the 2nd is an expansion of the first) or two narratives that are related by some other factor such as the use of quotation, but in any case, will be of the same text type.

The Stand Alone conference was more heavily dependent on repetition and allo-repetition of nominals and direct as opposed to the emulative indirect address than was the Transparent. Its lexical density, using the formula presented by Stubbs (see Biber 1988) was different. Lexical density is the proportion of lexical to grammatical words, a fundamental parameter of variation; its formula is: lexical density = 100 X L/N, where L=lexical items: N, Adj, Adv, MainVerb, and N=number of words (Stubbs 1996: 72). Texts present ranges in their lexical density; Stubbs notes that the ranges are "34 to 58 percent for spoken texts; and 40 to 65 percent for written texts" (73). In table 6.10, unique words refers to the words listed separately as if occurring only once; total words refers to the words in all their repetition. Grammatical or function words are auxiliary verbs, modal verbs, pronouns, prepositions, determiners, conjunctions; lexical words are nouns, main verbs, adjectives and adverbs.

Table 6.9. Modals, Public and Private Verbs, Qualifiers, and Negation, Stand Alone Entries 306, 309, 310, 315

Entry Number	Chunk 1	Chunk 2	Chunk 3	Chunk 4	Chunk 5	Chunk 6
306	private: learn/we should not (3)	just	private: believe private: know/3 private: have seen private: have heard	very private: know		not
309	private: believe/you priv: feel/you should not	private: believe/3 should not (3)	public: say private: hope			
310	absolutely completely public: agree	for sure can+neg public: say+neg	only can			
315	really private: know private: see	absolutely just feel like private: assumes/3 private: feel	private: thinks/e	could private: learn/3 private: realize/3		

Table 6.10. Lexical Density for Transparent Conference, Topic 2

Unique Words	= 1540	Total Words	= 6840
Unique Grammatical Words	= 81	Total Grammatical Words	= 2780
Unique Lexical Words	= 1459	Total Lexical Words	= 4060

This Notes-Topic from the Transparent conference is not an overwhelmingly "nominalized" text. Nouns represented 12% (12.44%) of the total words of the full corpus, and 21% (20.96%) of the lexical words.

Using Stubbs's formula for density,=100 X L/N, Notes-Topic 2 in the Transparent conference has a lexical density of 59.01, which is at the top of the range for a spoken text, and above the median for written text. However, the percentage for nouns shows that the density in this text is from verbs, adjectives, and adverbs; figures for downtoners, hedges, and emphatics are higher for this text than for the Stand Alone conference. Lexical density alone might suggest this text to be highly informational, but the amount of nominalization argues that we not be surprised by the presence of features that Biber's analyses demonstrate as showing involvement.

The Stand Alone conference was similar to the Transparent in terms of lexical density, with 59.6 percent. However, nominalization was slightly greater: nominals were 37.8 percent of the total for lexical words and 38.25 percent of the total for all unique words. In the Stand Alone conference, pronominal forms were more frequently repeated, which probably accounts for the slight difference in overall patterns. Grammatical words were 8.8 percent of unique tokens and 40.4 percent of total words; lexical words were 91.2 percent of unique tokens and 59.6 percent of total words.

Different groups of people engaged in the same task will present variation, just as individuals preserve and present their idiolect. Members of the Stand Alone conference had the possibility of seeing each other personally, while the Transparent participants were on two campuses. We should not be surprised, then, to see a slight rise in some features of modality with the Transparent conference, as these students may have felt the need for greater carefulness in presenting assertions, claims, and challenges.

Groups are composed of different individuals, who bring differing idiolects to a common task, who choose different features for repetition or emulation, and who preserve their own habits and preferences for rapid keyboard composition. On the surface, and examined from the perspective of characterizing how people use language in electronic discourse, certain commonalities emerge: people go back and forth between dimensions such as informational and involved, they present mixed genres of texts or alternate among text types, they vary the amount of direct or indirect address they offer. When we examine the discourse at the level of the individual, we see more intricate patterns and subtleties.

In Appendix A, Shandie's response from the Transparent Conference shows how the shifts in her discourse, marked for the analyst by TTR for each fifty-word segment, may have given signals to her immediate readers, her audience, not only about her shifts in topic, her degree of confidence, her ways of legitimating her own ideas, opinions and feelings, but also for where and how they might most easily respond to her text by chiming in.

7:// Aspects of emulation

Both electronic messages and electronic mail offer writers a chance to emulate each other, supported by the reply format and the subject header (Cooper and Selfe 1990). In electronic conference discourse, emulation, a form of repetition in which students imitate, appropriate, and adapt larger patterns of discourse, was one of the two ways individual writers both established and tested conference conventions for interaction. The students' emulation of each other's words, phrases, sentences, and rhetorical strategies was tied to their evolving notion of audience within the conference. Constructs such as "audience" can be affected by the ways asynchronous electronic conferences apparently readjust notions of space and time for their participants (Black, Levin, Mehan, and Quinn 1983). Through emulation, students indicate their awareness of audience across time and space.

Popularity and rhythm

In an electronic conference such as VAXNotes, which presents the participant with any number of what the software calls "topics" from one to many, the Notes-Topic a student chooses is located in space as well as time. A popular Notes-Topic, one whose initial text attracted a greater number of responses than other topics, would present readers with successively more text and a greater set of emulative possibilities. Its growing length might attract new readers/writers, so that the choice of Notes-Topic might in itself be a presequence to emulation. The first two Notes-Topics were the places that attracted the most entries in each of the three conferences we ran. Were these topics popular because they were at the beginning? Here beginning has a dual sense: these Notes-Topics were first in terms of historical time, or the original chronological order of publication for the newspaper texts, and first in terms of space, or the spatial ordering of conference Topics which paralleled the chronological.

There are several notions of time associated with asynchronous conferencing (Black, Levin, Mehan, and Quinn 1983). These include conference duration, or the length of time that a conference is open for participation; conference frequency, or the number of times that participants access the conference; individual duration, or the time spent in reading and writing each time a person enters the conference; and the individual frequency of a person's participation in the conference over the time it is open. One may also investigate time in the sense either of patternings of peaks of interactivity within the conference's duration, or the fine-tuned patternings of the individual days and hours that a participant signs onto a conference for reading and writing, keyed to the personal time frame of daily life for that participant. Any or all of these factors are in operation each time people log in and enter asynchronous conferences. There are doubtless other time- or space-bound distinctions, such as the time it takes individuals to learn the software, or to learn how to participate in the evolving norms of discourse within a conference.

The asynchronous conference preserves the trace of each visit for which the person chooses to leave a writing behind. Since all writing stays in the conference, a text can continue to have an effect even though its writer has departed. It is ultimately the text, as representing the writer, which has impact and sustains the conference. The Sit-Ins conferences presented an additional complication of time in that the newspaper texts presented in virtual time were from an earlier period of history, or recorded time. The students entered the conference in real time, the *now* time of the 1990s, to read and respond to materials from the 1960s. Their responses often dealt with their own history of themselves as well as a collective history, represented by the newspaper stories, shared by all the students.

A Notes-Topic within the conference, and the writings included within that Topic, while time-bound in terms both of clocks and of mental constructs, can also be seen in terms of their topography, or as places. The conference Notes-Topics offered landmarks and the suggestion of pathways in the uncharted spaces for the writing of replies. The participants could range throughout the conference, select a landmark Notes-Topic, and construct a reply. A series of replies could thus constitute a pathway or patterning of interest and participation, in terms of the written interaction of participants who chose to visit certain places or texts in that Topic. These replies left literal traces of the participants' visit behind them in the form of more text. Just as sociologists often examine friendship networks as part of their description of social organization, or literary critics examine citation or allusion to text as part of their study of its influence, the investigator of electronic conference discourse can look at popularity of a topic or at the thematic and discourse topics that developed within it as writers responded to each others' texts.

A Notes-Topic within the Sit-Ins conferences had its own rhythm There were generally two surges of interaction or flurries of interest, as suggested by the dates recorded by the software. This pattern held, whether we extended a conference for two weeks, four weeks, or six weeks. In order to test the impact of popularity, we looked at who visited which "place" (Notes-Topic) and in which order, for Topics with the most total entries in the 1990 UNCC Stand Alone conference, and then checked to see if and how the pattern was replicated in the Exchange and Transparent conferences. In each semester's conference, the first two Notes-Topics attracted the greatest number of writings by the time the conference closed; however, total number of writings is not the only way to describe the popularity of a Notes-Topic, because students were asked to post a minimum of four responses. Nearly half of the students chose to write in these two Topics for either their first or second postings. The remainder of the writings in these Topics were from third and fourth choices by just over half the students and from return visits, in which students had posted a question or provocative statement and returned to the topic later, to review responses and post further comments to other writers.

Did the day chosen by a student for first conference entry affect popularity? The notion of first day can have two senses, by conference and by student: the first day that the conference is opened to students, and the first day for each individual student as she or he enters the conference and writes a first response. We hypothesized that students might sign on to the conference and enter the first Topic (newspaper story) presented. Such was not the case: ten Notes-Topics were chosen by the fifteen students entering on the first day the Stand Alone conference was open. Although the first two Topics contained the most entries, and were thus the most popular, there may have been other factors affecting how students chose their place to begin writing in the conference.

There were generally two surges of interaction or flurries of interest in any conference. One of these flurries generally occurred a few days after the first group of students had entered the conference, and the other was generally a few days later. The second day of the conference was the second day that students actually entered and wrote in the conference, not necessarily the second day that the conference was open for entry. The first surge of interaction for the Stand Alone conferences came on the second day of student participation: nineteen postings by five students. Since some Topics now contained multiple responses, which offered several student-generated subtopics, and since participants could select and respond to any of these, what looked like a discussion began to occur. Student writers began to use direct and indirect address to each other's writings, such as a turn taking response to the immediately preceding posting in a Topic. While time of day doubtless had some influence on the writing of responses, its significance was unapparent: students could log on from any of several labs on campus and developed their own individual patterns for time of log-ins depending on which lab was closest to their habitual path across campus or on which lab had terminals available on any given day. In table 7.1, students sometimes appear to post at the same time; the software logged time to the second, so we have arranged these in chronological order.

In general, students writing more than one reply on any particular day generally spent half an hour between their first and final postings. Student 1 and student 5 illustrate this point. Student 1 signed on, browsed, and read for an indeterminate time, and posted a reply in Topic 8 at 3:31. Ten minutes later, #1 posted her second reply, in Topic 7, and fifteen minutes later, her third in Topic 5. Fourteen minutes later, she wrote her last reply, in Topic 16. Student 5's postings were five, eight, and seven minutes apart. The conference software recorded the students' activities within the

Table 7.1. Stand alone conference: Second day of student participation
(October 18, 1990)

Place (Topic)	Student Posting	Number in a Topic	Time
8	1	8.3	15:31
7	1	7.3	15:41
2	2	2.4	15:41
2	2	2.5	15:44
2	3	2.6	15:46
5	1	5.4	15:56
10	3	10.3	16:02
9	2	9.2	16:02
16	1	16.1	16:10
3	4	3.4	16:13
13	3	13.1	16:20
9	5	9.3	16:23
2	4	2.7	16:25
9	5	9.4	16:28
5	4	5.5	16:32
10	5	10.4	16:36
7	5	7.4	16:43
6	4	6.6	16:54

conference, in terms of the time a reply was posted, but not details such as the time a student actually logged on or the number of keystrokes or corrections made.

By the seventh day of participation in the Stand Alone conference, students had entered texts responding to each Notes-Topic in the conference; all remaining students had to function as respondents rather than initiators in a Notes-Topic. When we compared characteristics of persons initiating Notes-Topics, we found that gender and ethnic proportions remained roughly the same for every conference. For example, women were no more likely than men to act as initiators when proportions of initiators compared to total population were examined. Although gender may influence participation in a real time (synchronous) electronic exchange (Cooper and Selfe 1990; Michel 1992), it apparently does not have the same effect in asynchronous conferences, which specify a minimum number of responses about an assigned topic.

Moving to reflexive writing

At what point did students begin using language about language, or reflexive language (Lucy 1993b)? We had anticipated this sequence: first, a student would sign on for the first time, and, unfamiliar with the conference software, might express a brief response to the events mentioned in a particular newspaper story, perhaps elaborating that response in the second posting. Perhaps in response 3 or 4, the student might comment on features of language used in the newspaper story. And if the conference is read in a linear order—that is, reading every entry in the first Notes-Topic, proceeding to Topic 2, and so on—it is possible to see the rough shape of the sequence we had predicted. But like us, the reader might be wrong. The linear order for individual topics is not fully representative of what the students actually did.

Conference Notes-Topics whose initiator began writing in reflexive language were more likely to contain reflexive use of language throughout that topic. In other words, once a writer had opened a Notes-Topic by writing language about language, other writers were likely to emulate this focus. Generally, reflexive language, once initiated, established a thread of this type of discourse within a Topic. Several conference Notes-Topics, each short, were exclusively reflexive. If both the first and second student writings in any Topic were primarily reflexive, and if either of these were lengthy, then the thread, or topical chaining, of the next five entries was established through emulation. Unless someone's writing presented two styles—moving, for example, from reflections on language to personal disclosure—the Notes-Topic soon closed. There was no gender distinction in the patterns. Most students addressed the issue of language use. Many dealt with it more than once, and often began their series of writings with this focus.

It may be that the shorter conference topics were short because they were primarily reflexive: students had nothing with which to chime in unless they had noticed additional features of language beyond those mentioned in previous student postings. Popular Topics, like the conference itself, moved with their own rhythm. Postings of various lengths often mingled reflection with disclosure and interpretation of past or present events. Discourse threads or chains were recycled, and there were distinct flurries of direct-address interaction. Where the conference's surges of interaction were often keyed to time—that point at which there were enough student writings and enough students to engage each other's texts—the individual Topic's surges were more often keyed to spaces, as students wrote to each other's texts.

Emulation across distance and space in the transparent conference

When people quoted or referred to previous postings, how far back could they refer and expect to be understood? There seem to be limits on referential distancing in face-to-face or voice-to-voice conversation (Givón 1983a; Chafe 1986; Chafe and Danielewicz 1987). Conversation is evanescent; electronic conference postings are not, at least for the life of the conference. Two samples—of a single Notes-Topic running throughout the full time the conference was mounted, and of a single day's action across all Topics in the conference—show how the students accommodated conversational conventions to the medium of electronic discourse. In asynchronous conference texts, referentiality takes place in space rather than in time, for that is how the texts are arranged. Students evidently assumed they were being read, and signaled their readings of other writers through repetition or emulation, since they could not be assured that their reply to text no. 33 would appear in the program's list of writings as text no. 34.

In all three conferences, Topic 2 invariably attracted postings from the greatest number of students. Topic 2 was the first newspaper story about the Sit-Ins. Topic 1 presented the directions for the conference. In the Transparent conference, students joined that Topic on the first day the conference was opened and were still writing in it on the day the conferenc ended. The Transparent conference involved students from three classes on two campuses, which allowed a look at different kinds of interactions and audiences. Since the Topic had its own rhythm for peaks of activity in student writing, there were corollary peaks in the levels of interaction. As with the Stand Alone and Exchange conferences, the Transparent conference had two surges or peaks of activity (frequency and length of responses) with October 24 as the first peak of interaction involving students from both campuses. Two Notes-Topics in particular attracted students on this day: the heavily popular Topic 2, and the runner-up, Topic 4 (students also wrote responses in Topics 3, 8, 9, and 11).

For an analysis of interactivity and audience awareness, student writings were coded sequentially by order of posting, within their writers'class and campus cohorts. Each writing was scored on a five-point scale to identify referential cues:

1 – named/addressed a specific person by first or last name or userid
2 – named/addressed a specific writing by title or number
3 – presented a cue that writing is in context of previous writing by self or by others
4 – used a pronoun addressing Others—for example, "you," "we"
5 – presented Other audience-cuing, "broadcast" to all readers— for example, "some people"
0 – had no discernible address to audience.

Appendix C presents a correlation of frames of address and titles with schematicized narrative components for all entries on the single day of October 24. All of the entries on that day for topic 4 included frames of address either to "you" or "we" (#4 on the scale) or were broadcast to include all the student readers, with cues such as "some people" or "many writers" or "some people in my class" (#5 on the scale). Entries for Notes-Topic 2, on the other hand, had no such frames. Only one of the writings on October 24 was directed to a specific and named person (#1 on the scale). The other writings on that day included cues that presented indirect address, through several kinds of repetition: quotations marked or pointed by punctuation, unpointed quotations, morphological extensions of a lexical item (*field general/generals*), and so on.

As in the Stand Alone conference, Notes-Topics in the Transparent conference seemed to develop their own characteristic norms: the entries for October 24 from Topic 4 were typical for that topic. Nearly all entries in Topic 4 on any day used broadcasting to indicate audience or referent, and presented discourse about discourse, or reflexive writing (Lucy 1993b). The newspaper story that headed Topic 4 did not present reflexive writing. Student writers, while maintaining their own idiolectal preferences for register shifts, titles, and preferred correlations of syntactic with lexical repetition and rhetorical strategy, were emulating the framing, the stance, and the focus of their peers.

Adjacency pairs in the transparent conference

The notion of referential distance—or how "far away" in space and time one can get before losing the thread of the discourse—is stretched within electronic discourse, particularly if it is at all hypertextual, as the Appendix B for October 24 shows in greater detail. Two other aspects round out the picture: the contiguity of the adjacency pairing for turns in oral conversation, and the kinds of referentiality presented by direct and indirect address. Direct address, as its name implies, is writing specifically directed to another, named, text or its writer, the written equivalent of "Hey, you!, Blake, this is for you." Indirect address is usually effected by repetition and emulation, allowing writers to chime in to writings by others. Analysis of the forty-seven entries in topic 2 showed some interesting correlations between the type of title devised by the student writers and their uses of direct and indirect address to other writings or writers. In table 7.2, writings whose titles presented some sort of discourse signature are classified as group 1. The titles of group 2 presented no such signature.

All but two entries presented personal disclosure of thoughts, feelings, opinions, and memories, usually prefixed by "I." Indirect address to another writer or writing was presented in some way by every posting in the conference. But with one exception, only the

Table 7.2. Discourse signature

	Writings		*Writings*
Group 1:	35	Group 2:	12
Titling game	20	Newspaperlike headline:	10
Initials of name	4	Blank (no title)	2
First/last name	8		
Numbered answer	2		
Directive	1		

writers in group 1 directly addressed each other, as shown in the table 7.3. The "ringer" in group 2 was a writing that began with a direct response in first-person to a specified writer of a preceding writing; though the entry bore the headlinelike title "Racism and Christianity," the entry was in every other way like the writings in group 1. The majority of writers in that group moved into reflexive discourse about either the words or the style of the newspaper story. Nearly every instance of what we are calling adjacency pair reference occurred in writings by this group.

The only confident way to determine adjacency pairing is if the two entries are adjacent in the same topic, and the second includes either direct or indirect address, as when Donna's entry, 2.03, includes "I agree with Spud and Nora" (entries 2.01 and 2.02). Chronological time cannot help here: Donna posted her entry several days later. Other students had preceded Donna's entry into the conference but had posted replies in other Topics. When we move away from a strict interpretation of adjacency pairing—that is, the notion that it is two successive remarks in voice-to-voice conversation—

Table 7.3. Adjacency pairs

	Group 1	Group 2
Addressed by name specific writer/writing	9	1
Cue that writing is in context of previous writing by self/other (indirect address)	27	1
Used pronoun for other or broadcast to all: "you," "we," "some"	5	0
Marked quotation from or allusion to specific writing	23	1
Adjacency pair reference to immediately preceding writing	10	1

we begin to see the complexities in establishing referential distancing and in discerning emulation within asynchronous conferencing.

Frames of address to other writers or postings throughout topic 2 presented considerable variation. Twenty-seven of the forty-six replies presented such frames, with ten of those including either direct address to, or punctuation-marked quotation from, the immediately preceding posting. Using the distance between postings, as signaled by posting numbers, for establishing a mean, median, and range of deviation for referential distance was, however, misleading. Students entered the conference wherever they wished, and read until they felt like writing. The writer of posting 2.42, for example, who began with "What kind of name is Spud, anyhow?" quite possibly did not read all forty-one of the preceding replies, but stopped after reading the first one, entitled "Spud speaks," to enter her posting. The writer of posting 2.18, who quoted directly from posting 2.03, may have read the previous seventeen postings, or 2.01–2.03, or, attracted by 2.03's title in the Notes-Topic listing, she may have entered the conference with 2.03 and written her reply at that point.

Based on the evidence of postings, which both referenced or addressed the immediately preceding entry and an earlier one as well, it looks as if students evidently read an average of five to seven entries. Six of the postings in Topic 2 evidenced this by addressing or quoting postings that were two, four, three, eight, eight and eighteen entries away. If we take no fewer than five, no greater than seven as our average, frames of address to distant postings are explained as being where the writer stopped reading and started writing. Patterns of emulation take on a conversationlike rhythm of their own. The entry "Donna's turn" illustrates frames of direct address as well as how student writers used intertextual references, quotations, and emulation of pattern to substitute for conversation's adjacency pairs and turn taking. As Donna's posting was the most frequently addressed or referenced throughout the conference, we cite it in full:

2.02 Donna's turn

I agree with Spud and Nora; the situation described in this article makes my blood run cold. However, in response to Nora's observation about the style, I cannot agree. In most newspaper articles I read these days, I get the distinct impression that the article supports one side of the issue versus the other; in fact, many conservative politicians these days feel that the media is unfair to them, that the media is nothing more than a bunch of "bleeding-heart liberals." I will not reveal my politics here, but will say that I see nothing wrong with the way the media treats conservative politicians. Anyway, to get back to the article, I DO agree with Nora's observation about the tone of the article, relative to its historical context. It IS very surprising to find an article sympathetic to the Civil Rights Movement in a southern newspaper at that time.

Frame and focus in topic 2

Talking about intertextuality among written texts is much like talking about issues of referentiality in conversation. In the forty-six postings of Notes-Topic 2, referentiality was also effected by the ways the student writers emulated each other's choice of subtopic or elaboration of an issue. When students moved into reflexive commentary or discourse about discourse, we noted whether they were writing about words or style. When they wrote about events reported in or associated with the newspaper story, we charted whether they were talking about the events in general (unmarked: "the Sit-Ins" in the story) or the events and their import "at that time" (the sixties) or "in that place" (the south; Greensboro and Charlotte). Since nearly every entry presented personal disclosure of ideas, thoughts, opinions, or events in its writer's life, we classified that as the unmarked or expected vehicle. We distinguished it from personal response, which was a statement of emotional reaction to either the events in the newspaper story or to comments made by other writers in the conference.

Topical chaining in the conventional sense of (linear) development over time (Martin 1992) or topic flow (Shuy 1990) can be demonstrated for electronic conference discourse, but must be adapted for a nonlinear reading because students could enter the conference at any topic, with any posting, and reply at any time. The linear order of student postings in a Notes-Topic is an approximation of chronological reality for interaction within that Topic, but not of the full interaction going on in the whole conference itself.

The short list in table 7.4 of the strategies, subtopics, or issues that arose as students read each other's postings, is just that, a list. It cannot necessarily be assumed from this list that because one issue was raised in posting number seven and another in posting eleven, that the writer of posting eleven had read and was emulating or elaborating on anything from number seven unless direct address or repetition provided additional substantiation. For the writer of posting eleven could have been emulating and elaborating posting number ten, and ten could have been emulating number seven—or could have transferred a gist with strategies, issues, subtopics, or lexical items from participating in another, completely different topic a few minutes before writing number ten.

Emulation usually ran through five to seven postings, with a new subtopic or strategy being introduced between the fourth and seventh, after which a second cycle began. Once a subtopic or strategy had been introduced, subsequent writers could chime in to it at any time. And a posting might include more than one subtopic or strategy. The writings in the Transparent conference nearly always included more than one, because, we think, of the students' sense of audience. A good example is the ways students projected

Table 7.4. Strategies and subtopics in order of appearance in Topic 2, transparent conference

Subtopic	Entry Number	
Personal response to newspaper story	1	
Reflexive writing about words in the story	2	
Reflexive writing about style of the story		
Events "at that particular time"	3	
Events "in that particular place"		
"In my country" cultural parallels	4	
My memory of those events	7	
Projection: what I might have done then	13	
My friends as part of my history of response	16	[variation on "memory"]
My age during those events	17	[variation on "memory"]
Other cultures in the US	18	[variation on "in my country"]
Religious issues	20	
Media in general	28	
Writers for the media: their responsibility	30	
Color terms as terms for ethnic groups	34	
Gender issues	36	

themselves back into the past, to question what they might have done at that time. Projection was introduced in writing 13; writings 14–17 also projected themselves into the past, and writer 17, who responded directly to 16, added comments about her own age during the sixties. Writer 18 picked up the thread of cultural parallels, which had last been mentioned in writing 5; writer 19 returned to projection, and 20, who responded directly to 19, both projected and introduced the issue or subtopic of religion. Projection was again used in writings 24, 28, 29, and 33, which also discussed different aspects of the media and the responsibility of writers for the media. Here, projection not only placed the reader back in time, it offered a way for the writers to discuss whether the newspaper reporter reflected racism in the society of the 1960s without necessarily alienating other participants in the multiracial conference of the 1990s.

Some features of audience in the transparent conference

The Transparent conference involved twenty UNC-Greensboro students and forty-seven UNC-Charlotte students in two sections, twenty-five in one and twenty-two in the other. The students were aware that they wrote for an audience whom they did not know personally and probably could not meet in a face-to-face situation, and for whom they had no age, gender, or ethnic cues to rely upon except as those were self-disclosed in the entries. Writers of entries could not, then, assume that any problems of interpretation could be smoothed out in personal interaction and could also not assume that other student reader/writers would be able to immediately understand their references. Students writing in the Transparent conference had different constraints on their ways of formulating gist, since their receptive audience was larger and more impersonal than the audiences in the Stand Alone and Exchange conferences. Their ways of social cuing, or enculturation, differed as well.

Even though the students in the Exchange conference knew in advance that their writings would be exchanged with the other class for response, as they read and wrote, they did so within the cultural space of "our class." In the Transparent conference, students had the cultural space of "our campus," but not necessarily "our class."

They had not exchanged autobiographical introductions or proffered other forms of greeting. A desire for direct, familiar, personalized interaction may have been the impetus behind the language
play of the Titling Game (see chapter 4).

The teacher prompt for the conferences had stipulated that students write and post a minimum number of responses. In every
conference, some students wrote more than the minimum. In the
Stand Alone conference,the extra writings usually presented additional rhetorical strategies or a change of style for a particular writer.
In the Transparent conference, however, the additional writings were
in almost every case a postscript: an afterthought, a clarification, or
an insight left unfinished in the reply just posted. They usually
followed chronologically upon the heels of the previous posting.
Females and males were equally likely to add these postscripts,
which carried direct reference to the text just written and displayed
the writer's sense of audience with comments that in a play would
be called an "aside."

Roughly half the students who wrote all their entries either on
a single day, or in two visits within a four-day period, wrote at least
one entry longer than 150 words. Students posting entries over a
longer span of time, from a week apart to throughout the conference, were more likely to write two or more postings of more than
150 words. If a student chose to enter the conference at several
different times, the student also wrote lengthier postings. This could
be because there were more writings by other students available to
read, or because there were shifts in the flow of the discussions to
note, or because these were people who enjoyed writing longer
responses and were also intrigued by some aspect of the conference
conversation.

The writers who wrote multiple entries throughout the full time
the Transparent conference was mounted did not have the "last word."
Since the conference was asynchronous, writers, unlike speakers, did
not need to bid for the floor. The writers of multiple entries simply
had more to say. And since their writings were seldom directly addressed by other students, they may have written too much, raising
the issue of whether there might be some sort of preferred length,
which would attract the response of other readers/writers in the conference. Writers who posted multiple responses over the full time
period of the conference usually presented philosophically rooted

arguments for their text-based commentary, positions, or beliefs, and were less likely to present personal experience. Perhaps this way of writing, or the particular philosophies outlined, presented too few places into which other writers could chime. At any rate, philosophical mediation with little affect or disclosure was a pattern that was seldom emulated.

In general, the writings in the Transparent conference were longer than the writings in either the Stand-alone or the Exchange conference, with three times as many writings of 150 words than in the other two. This length was sustained in the Transparent conference of fall 1993 as well, which suggests that the mental construct of audience plays a significant role in a multiparty conference. In e-mail lists, some writers post more frequently and also post longer replies: if one reads an electronic list for several months, one begins to associate length with the directory listing of one writer's userid, wit with another's, and so on.

However, a conference presents different conventions for reference. Since all the postings for the history of the entire conference are always retrievable, the writer does not have to present lengthy quotations ("On January 8, userid X at this address said: . . . ") In a conference where the participants think they might know each other or could know each other in a face-to-face setting, referentiality and cohesion become almost a shorthand, as all of the writers share texts, prompts, and each other's postings. In a multiparty conference, where the option of social interaction in face-to-face settings is neither possible nor feasible, varying the length of responses may be one substitute mechanism for handling a desire for social contact on a personal level. People were simply at greater pains to explain themselves.

In the Transparent conference, students incorporated multiple frames within a single writing. Where the writers in the Stand Alone and Exchange conferences usually worked with two frames per entry, and presented reflexive discourse about specific language use in a separate entry, writers in the Transparent conferences mixed three or more. They mingled three or more frames for personal reaction, examples from personal experience, evaluation of the newspaper text's tone, genre, and bias, assessment of the newspaper or reporter's intent, projection of themselves into the events of that time, and reflexive language.

Flocking behaviors in mainframe conferences

Discussions of emulation or repetition have often suggested that when people quote, repeat, or allude to the writings of others, their writings are somehow deficient or boring, and hence dismissable. Emulation in an electronic conference is actually a primary social construct to demonstrate that the writer has read, has remembered, and may even be aligning with a previous writing or writer's viewpoint. We prefer Tannen's use of "allo-repetition," and take it further with what we call "chiming." In electronic conference discourse, a successful posting—what we might be tempted to call a competent performance—presents a chord. Other readers or writers can add their burden to either the fundamental frequency or to any of the harmonics. These are their performances in writing, which can be most successful on the basis of the nature rather than the frequency with which other writers chime in.

Choosing which entry or entries to read is a selection strategy involving some aspects of prediction and confirmation; choosing which elements to repeat—be they from the morphology, the lexicon, the frames, the parts of the narrative, the affective or text-based strategies of legitimation and self-authorization, the discourse strategies keyed to genre—these, too, are cognitively driven, tied to gist-formation, and selected within a social complex that involves the norms known outside the conference and those that develop within it. A chime of bells is a repetitive, recursive patterning; to chime in is an act that aligns the new ringer of chimes within the overall pattern discerned, hypothesized, projected. It is here, with the double sense of chiming, that the metaphor becomes explanatory, even theoretical.

Writers in electronic conferences such as the ones we study here do not stay with the same topic. They transfer the new material which has become a given or shared topos within one topic to the new one they visit. We suspect the building process of shared information works like the coral reef, built in a fractal formation (where ontology recapitulates phylogeny) as opposed to a linear mode alone. In short, they flock. In single group constructs, they range more widely across topics. In multiparty constructs, they flock in clumps: it is as if they have a different range, a different set of landmarks, a different set of pathways keyed to their sense of flock-ness. In single group constructs, they can see each other. In multiparty constructs, they are flying blind, paralleled by one or more flocks whom they cannot see and whom they do not want to jostle from the flight patterns being established.

We realize that moving from a musical to an avian metaphor can be confusing, but we have done this deliberately. The musical metaphor presents the multiplicity of hierarchical choices; the avian metaphor reminds us of the patterns we can sense, describe, but cannot necessarily predict at the outset. The kinds of computational discourse modeling presented by Biber (1988, 1994) and the text or corpus models provided by van Dijk and Kintsch (1983) and others are both needed when looking at the complexities of interactive, multiparty, asynchronous discourse. It is here that several different approaches to text and discourse analysis can be highly useful for interpreting the written performances of electronic discourse.

In any case, the participants in an electronic conference do not stay still. We have checked this flocking behavior informally, in reviewing the kinds of behaviors presented on other conferences and closed lists we have set up for classes. In a class on Chaucer for undergraduates and graduates, students were enjoined to report and respond to five topics that were known ahead of time, and were mounted two weeks apart. Within these topics, mounted on a different mainframe as a closed list (as opposed to a conference), student writers generally stayed within the topic setup, but continued to save and post additions to favored topics: a sort of flocking.

In monitoring their own behaviors while reading exchanges on scholarly discussion lists, students reported themselves as threading topics—once they had discovered what the topic was—and simply signing off the list when the online discussion group moved to include new issues, unless they had found something within the quality of the group discussions to keep reading regardless of the topic announced in the subject headers. Conferences, with their ever-present archival capability, present topics that do not end: there is always room for another entry. An electronic conversation can go on only so long. After that period of time its interaction may be repeated or reintroduced, but seldom with the same intensity.

In electronic discourse, the reader/writer moves on both the synchronic and diachronic planes, using both hierarchical and networking processes, yet maintaining idiosyncratic idiolectal preferences. The phenomenon of language contact, even in a situation as ephemeral as a short-term electronic conference, is multiplex and confusing. After it has ended, just as when we were involved in its interaction, we read the conference in multiple ways.

8:// Emulating a strategy: The rhetorical question

One of the more fascinating aspects of the conferences was the way students manipulated rhetorical questions in order to achieve social and rhetorical connections with each other. The rhetorical question, as such, is closely allied in its underlying form with the tag, or yes-no question, which attaches a question to a statement, such as "Jane is going to the movie—isn't she?" The recipient of the question can answer with either a yes or a no, to confirm or disconfirm whether Jane is, indeed, going to the movie.

Rhetorical questions may be posed so that their recipient—the audience—could answer with yes or no. Depending on how they are scaffolded, these questions can also invite answers such as yes but, yes and no, and moreover or no but. The recipient of the rhetorical question, if human, animate, and awake, is not, however, expected to proffer the answer out loud: instead, the person asking the question is the one who is sanctioned to speak the answer, if there is one, on behalf of the recipient. A further distancing of the recipient to the role of audience takes place when the purported addressee is inanimate or is in some way unable to answer, as in apostrophes such as—O Moon, why does my love not love me? O Death, where is thy sting? O Long-departed, O Truth, O Hell. In some instances, the question is unanswerable, and the audience for the question is invited to ponder with the questioner the enigma, the irony, the catastrophe, or the paradox that has been presented.

Rhetorical questions are tricky, because though they are in question form, and call for an answer, they establish a different set of roles for the speaker/questioner and the respondee, roles keyed to the particular situation in which the question is posed and the

141

likelihood of an answer. A taxonomy of rhetorical questions would need to include whether the question was sure to entail an answer, likely to entail one, possibly to entail one, not likely to entail one, or under no foreseeable or felicitous circumstances to entail an answer. Their complexity lies not in their form, but in their illocutionary force, which can be that of an assertion, a prediction, an apology, a request, a directive. In short, the rhetorical question is a formulaic act that presents the full panoply of direct and indirect speech acts. The problem for the recipient—and in the case of electronic discourse, the reader—is to distinguish the question asking for information that is expected to be given by the respondee from the question asked with another purpose in mind.

Rhetorical questioning is, it seems to us, a fairly conscious technique adopted by a speaker for deliberate ends, and it is used infrequently, proportional to the length of the dialogue, oration, or conversation. We have no way of comparing their occurence and frequency in the computer conferences with face-to-face conversations by the students who participated. Our impression is that students seldom spoke rhetorical questions unless presenting some sort of set piece designed to sway the opinions of others, to intimidate or challenge, or to maintain control of a discourse. In the conferences, once the strategy of posing a rhetorical question was introduced into a topic, it was frequently emulated by successive writers, for a variety of rhetorical purposes. We think that the use and frequency of rhetorical questions in the conferences was a major way for students to present affect and to establish their own credibility. In that sense, rhetorical questioning was a way that students adapted conversational conventions to enculturate each other into wordings they would be willing to accept from each other.

Features of rhetorical questions

We analyzed the first twenty-five questions in the Stand Alone and Transparent conferences. The Exchange conference replicated the Stand Alone in its primary format, and the questions fell into similar categories. During the period when the two conferences were exchanged across campuses, students posed few questions of any kind, since there would be no way to solicit replies for information, and there was but limited time to read the responses from the other campus. The Stand Alone and Transparent conferences were differently situated, with students in the Transparent conference showing their awareness of unknown as well as known (or potentially knowable) writers.

We analyzed such features as the location of the question, the types of expectations for answers, and whether the answer was direct or indirect.

(1) *Location of question.* Was it initial, medial, or final in a posting or in a paragraph or frame within a posting? Where did it come in a sequence of postings to a particular topic?

Looking at location gave us a sense of how much staging, scaffolding, or planning led up to or away from a question. Location also interacted with how the writer included the reader in the sequence of mental or verbal acts that could be expected to follow a question. For example, questions that closed a full posting dispensed with the writer's opportunity to answer the question and frequently asked the reader to join with the writer in appreciating irony, paradox, or enigma, but left any successive acts of disagreement or agreement up to the reader.

Questions opening a frame or a posting were infrequent: apparently a norm within electronic discourse is for the writer to establish credibility for self or writer's viewpoint before posing a question. The most common location was medial within a frame or a posting, which allowed the writer to create a scaffolding for the reader who could use it to create a predictive strategy. Location within a particular topic played a role as well. In general, four to six sequential postings had to occur within a topic before any question, and especially a rhetorical question—that is, one that did not sincerely solicit verifiable fact or information from readers—could be posed. The scaffolding, which ranged from introductory adverb clauses through one to three sentences, allowed the writer a range of prefatory acts such as deferral, demurral, mitigation, or hedging, and other positive and negative face-saving verbal acts. The presence or absence of a scaffolding presented one set of cues to the reader about whether the question being asked was *real* or rhetorical, and what kind of answer might be expected.

(2) *Expectations for answers.* First, we looked at whether the question could be answered by any, some, or all readers in the

conference. Next, we charted whether the question and its scaffolding (or lack thereof) presented cues for the potential answer to be (a) affirmative or negative in the case of questions set up like tag-questions, or (b) a longer chain anticipated, as with either-or or if-then questions. If a question could be answered, the writer could be seen as seeking consensus. If the question was answered by the writer, then the reader could infer that the writer was establishing some kind of ownership for that answer. If the question was located frame- or posting-final, the writer usually presented irony or paradox (what Kertzer 1989 calls *enigma*; see Ilie 1994 for an extended discussion of rhetorical functions across a corpus of print media).

Affirmative answers included yes, yes-and; negative answers included no, no-and. Yes-but and no-but answers presented greater ambiguity. Modal verbs or anticipatory *it* in a yes-no question usually signaled the anticipated or projected affirmative response: can, do, has/had there become. Negative responses were cued with negation markers such as not, never, and occasionally by punctuation or capitalization suggesting an intonation contour (see example 2.23c, below). When a question was presented as an either-or choice, the unmarked or conventional response—to judge from those immediately followed by the writer's choice—was the second, unless some sort of elaborated scaffolding, fronting, extrapolation, or other signal was presented to the reader; see example 3.04, below. If-then questions were least questionlike, and least often seen. Their weight comes from the reader's perceiving how the writer establishes the if-argument and the then-consequence, and being invited to assent to that chain.

Roughly half the questions in each conference signaled the reader to assent or disagree, and if not occurring in frame or posting-final position, were usually answered for the reader by the writer, either directly or indirectly. With an indirect answer, of course, the reader is presented with affect in a more face-saving way for both reader and writer. Twenty percent of the questions in the Stand Alone conference presented the reader with either-or or if-then questions; this rose to 40 percent in the Transparent conference. We think this signifies the different sense of audience in that conference, with a wider range of mental speech acts projected onto the larger audience of known and unknown readers.

One category of questions arose in the Transparent conference, and did not occur in either the Stand Alone or the Exchange conferences: we are calling it the *aside*. This is a question that can have an answer, but probably represents a different speech act, such as an apology. Writers usually signaled these with parentheses, but the verb forms or punctuation signaling intonation indicate a direct address and often suggest expostulation.

(3) *The provision of an answer to a question.* Here we looked at whether the writer answered the question in the following phrase, clause, or sentence, and whether the answer was direct or indirect.

And of course, some questions were so framed that they could be interpreted as both yes-no and longer chains. If they are anything, rhetorical questions are multiply ambiguous, and their use in electronic discourse provides writers with greater flexibility and a wider range of speech acts just as it provides readers with more places to chime into the discussion—and to misread the writer's posting.

Rhetorical questions from the stand alone conference

These examples from the Stand Alone conference show the range and typify the uses for rhetorical questions among participants who know or have the potential to know each other. They highlight the way rhetorical questions were intertwined with aspects of direct and indirect address, and their role in establishing common ground or consensus for shared or given knowledge. We have chosen to display these questions in the order of Notes-Topics within the conference, to indicate their range. Within the Topics, as the strategy is emulated, one can have a sense of their intertextuality.

2.23 a. Looking back, we can see how wrong they were, but can we recognize our own bias and shortcomings? While it is good to recognize accomplishments, it is also necessary to acknowledge our faults if we are to progress.

The introductory adverbial phrase provides minimal scaffolding: "that was then; we are here now." The next sentence repeats the dual clause structure and reverses it, with an indirect answer in which the "our biases and shortcomings" of sentence one are equivalent to "our faults," which we must ("it is also necessary to") acknowledge.

b. Why were these two people arrested? I want to know.

Wh-structures are not enough of a cue for readers to be able to distinguish "real questions" from rhetorical ones. Here the writer underscores with the next sentence that he or she doesn't know the answer and that the question is sincere.

c. "They were closely pursued by police who kept order but did not attempt to divert the march." PLEASE. Water bombs and verbal harassment constitute order?

Note here how the writer adapts both *textual and conversational conventions* to create changes in meaning. A quotation from the newspaper story, indicated by the quotation marks, is followed by an all-caps PLEASE, which, since there is no request attached (hence breaking the maxim of quantity), signals irony—as in "Excuuuse me," or "Give me a break!" The use of all-caps can also indicate a raised voice, and is the conventional equivalent in e-mail of "shouting" which, as an infelicitous act in conversation again underscores that the student writer is using irony or suggesting negation. The question-mark at the end of the last sentence again reverses the declarative form and, like the intonational cue with the all-caps, suggests an intonation contour coupling question and irony.

3.04   No one has commented on the use of Negro (rather than black). Do we assume this as historical fact rather than curious, and perhaps offensive oddity?

Location of the question has impact here; it is the last line of the posting. Audience is invoked by the "we." The reader is given an indirect *either-or* choice, with the first choice marked as the preferred one by the "rather than" introducing the second clause. The writer has indicated her own stance toward the usage (a reflexive act of discourse) with the paired and slightly mitigated adjectives. An answer can be anticipated: yes, we will assume this to be historical fact *and* probably also assume it, with the writer, to be offensive.

3.06 a. Charles Mxxx and Anthony Lxxx are from JCSU and friends of mine. Do they know the history of their own predecessors? As a friend I did not ask.

This example demands *real-world knowledge* from its readers as well as the retention of information from the newspaper story. JCSU, Johnson C. Smith University, is a predominantly black university; the role of JCSU students in the 60s is a feature of the newspaper story. Both Mxxx and Lxxx may be presumed to be black and, according to the writer's answer, may not be aware of JCSU's role. The expected answer here, signaled by the negation in the sentence following the question, is "No: No, these two probably don't know the history of their school's participation in the early sit-in movement or the identity of the black students named in the story, as the writer was unwilling to embarass them or herself by asking a question that could cause them to lose face with her or with each other or with themselves." Here, scaffolding before and after the question, pointing in one direction to real-world knowledge and in the other, to the writer's assumptions, is necessary to understand the point behind the question which the writer is now sharing with multiracial readers.

b. Passive resistance is an option—Martin Luther King preached it and practiced it. Isn't it scary the humane thing to do is not always the popular thing to do anymore?

Here real-world or cultural knowledge assumed by the writer as shared by the readership interacts with the location of the question and a series of *nested propositions*. The writer expects readers to know King's rise to prominence grows during this time, for he is not cited in the newspaper story. The question, coming as the last line of the posting, uses a negative anticipatory-*it* construction coupled with the notion of fear, to present an aphoristic flavor and to lead the readership to say a series of yesses: yes, humane action is not necessarily popular action; yes, that paradox is frightening; and yes, the humane action is preferable. The writer saves face for self and readers with the "anymore," a suggestion that at an earlier time it might have been popular to be humane. Earlier in the posting, the writer had praised civil disobedience as a peaceful activity, and here equated passive resistance with humane behavior. The "isn't it scary" clause also puts the reader in a dilemma, as the nested clauses seem to contain something like a syllogism, and the reader must work backwards from the end of the sentence to unravel the series of claims.

3.09 a. QXY, What does one's skin color have to do with working toward basic human rights for all people? It should not matter whether you feel that discrimination against a certain group of people effects you personally or not. You either believe in human rights or you don't.

Direct address and a challenge are presented in the opening sentence of this posting; that the question is at least partly rhetorical but also open to counter-challenge as a "real" question is suggested by the indirect answer that follows in the next two sentences. Audience involvement is initiated with the "should" in the second sentence, which is underscored by the "you." Skin color doesn't have anything to do with working toward basic human rights— well, at least it "should not." The reader of this posting can participate in its intertexuality within the conference through its title, "If I Were Black?" Here, as in 2.23b, punctuation signals first a quotation and then an ambiguous intonational contour.

The writer is quoting a phrase from a previous student posting, and adding the question mark to a collocation that otherwise would not be read as a question. The posting is a direct reply to the student who had originally written "if I were black, I would. . . . " Given the direct address to the student, followed by a should prescription, and that the title would be the last item written, the reader can infer that the title is both a question and an additional expression, which could be facetious, ironic, confrontational, or angry. If readers wanted to find the posting being challenged, they could type DIR, and accessing the directory, use the student's userid to locate and read the entry. This may have been what the writer of the next posting did, as he or she rose to defend the original writing in her opening line: "I completely agree with QXY."

3.10 a. I completely agree with QXY. Its absolutely incredible that it could be so easily forgotten that blacks are human beings. Had their perception of a people they had beaten down so much become so twisted that they never stopped and thought for one minute that they were committing atrocities against their fellow man? Its hard to imagine such a time and it is always easy to say what you would have done, given the b. opportunity. I can't say for sure, how can anyone? I, of course hope I would have been one of those to have risked arrest. . . .

Here, each question addresses a different aspect of how its writer interpreted the preceding posting, in the dual context of the posting being challenged and the writer's own values. Each question has a *dual scaffolding or staging*, framing two different but interconnected, embedded narratives. The first question chimes the outrage and disbelief recorded in QXY's posting and intensifies it with adverbs "absolutely," "so easily," and with nouns with strong affect, "atrocities." The second question mitigates the claim of 3.09's writer by recontextualizing it within a context that casts doubt on anyone's ability to project their behavior after the event. The "answer" continues the mitigation with "of course hope."

3.11 a. By noting Jones' denials of what Covington deems to be obvious truth, the reporter plants a prejudicial seed in the readers' minds. Can the readers be sure of the truthfulness of anything that Jones or his followers say in the rest of the article? We are. . . .

In the first of three questions, each concerned with metadiscourse in the news story prompt, 3.11 uses the *unnegated modal deems* (plus adverb) to point readers—included in the "we are" sentence following the question—to choose the negative response while still maintaining a face-saving politeness by leaving room for doubt.

b. I wonder about the use of "darkened." Were counters darkened by the removal of artificial light at midday, or by the color of the demonstrators' skin?

Again, 3.11 uses the news story for his scaffolding; here, with a *quotation*, he sets up an either-or question, which carries at least two levels of meaning. Real-world knowledge assumes that artificial light, also used to signal that an establisment was open for business, would probably not be needed at midday and the skin color of demonstrators in this story was black. 3.11 uses this assumption to shift the terms of the definition and project an indirect claim that people at the time of the Sit-Ins, including the writer of the news story, were highly prejudiced against people of color.

> c. . . . reporter also made the statement that "The students themselves were orderly. . . . " Why would this creep even add such a comment? My only answer is that he automatically thinks that the students would be loud and obnoxious. He also probably. . . .

Wh-questions are evidently seen by their writers as ambiguous in electronic discourse. A wh-question, particularly a "why-," could as easily be a "real" question as a rhetorical one. Here, 3.11 signals that he is using the wh- or why-question as a platform for his own opinion in the next sentence, and that he is going beyond simple expostulation.

> 3.19 a. b. Another thing that bothered me was the word "negro." I felt that to be just as bad as nigger. To me the word makes me thoroghly (sp? my brains dead?) sick to my stomach. Being as narrow-minded as to close a lunch counter just. . . .

This final example of the range of uses for rhetorical questions in the Stand Alone conference illustrates the rhetorical question that is *probably an apology*. The writer is unsure of the spelling of "thoroughly," is reasonably confident that it is misspelled, and flags this with "sp?," as a way to say "Is this spelled correctly? It may not be," followed immediately with a statement and question: "my brains dead?" Here, an approximate translation might be "I'm tired and I think my brain may be dead, for I can no longer spell correctly: Is the word misspelled and has my memory and thinking ability completely collapsed? I think certainly the first is true and am apologizing by proffering the second question as an excuse."

Rhetorical questions in the transparent conference

The major changes of interaction differentiating the Transparent conference from the Stand Alone conference are suggested by the different patterns in number and use of rhetorical questions. In general, the writers in the Transparent conference also used rhetorical questions to insert affect, to include audience in an apparent search for consensus or to establish authority. They were more apt to present either-or questions, which, though the writer often "answered" with her or his own set of preferences and values, were designed to include the reader or audience in a sustained chain of inferences and, occasionally, syllogistic reasoning. And again, the use of modals, adverbs, and negation features often pointed the reader to identify the writer's preference in an either-or or if-then series. These two examples show both the *direct* and the *indirect* ways that students established such chains:

> T2.29   If I had been raised in the sixties what would my reaction to the sit-ins have been? Would I have been willing to help the blacks in their protest against the restaurant or would I have been one of the many who stood back and watched it happen? I don't know that I have an answer to that question. I have never been faced with a situation even remotely. . . .
>
> T2.37   It infuriates me to think that someone thinks a restaurant is a private place of business. Plainly, food service is a public industry. But then I guess that's what the students at the sit-in were trying to say, huh?

Students in the Transparent conference were also more apt to use rhetorical questions as exclamation or expostulation. They frequently quoted or replied directly to each other, as in these two examples focusing on the news story's author:

> T3.10   . . . i wasn't even born then and I realize that. Where was this man, on the moon?

> T3.13   I agree with Suzanne who wrote "where was
> this man, on the moon?" Anyone who has any
> idea of what was actually going on in the world
> knows that the protestors would have gotten
> nowhere following the "proper channels. . . . "

The writers in the Transparent conference often used rhetorical questions, as in the examples above, to outline their notions of what was or what should be (from their perspective) a common, given, shared knowledge. Establishing common ground is, we think, more difficult when writers know they do not and probably cannot know all of the other writers. Rhetorical questions function as a fairly overt means of negotiation and community formation. In the Stand Alone conference, rhetorical questions certainly played the same role, but the questions in the Transparent conference were longer, their staging more elaborate, and their answers, furnished either by the original writer or in a direct reply from a peer, were equally amplified.

Another technique of achieving some consensus or community with the expanded audience that enveloped writers in the Transparent conference was the direct address to that audience, sometimes with a directly-addressed inclusive you, occasionally as an inclusive we, and frequently as an unspecified "aside." These examples illustrate the ways students addressed their readership.

a. *No specification*

> T2.18   The tone of this article is actually a bit hopeful.
> I got this wonderful vision of a group of stu-
> dents convinced of their innate "rightness" [does
> that make sense?]. . . . Need I say that I am
> white?
>
> T2.37   But then I guess that's what the students at the
> sit-in were trying to say, huh?

b. *Generic specification*

> T3.10   i got lost in trying to keep up with the meaning
> of the words so the meaning of the article had

no bearing on what i was reading. does that make
sense to anyone else but me?

c. *Interlink between no specification and generic specification:
a two-step chain*

T4.01 Gee, what about letting these people eat at the
lunch counter? That might work! It's very hard
to be analytical about these articles: the subject
matter is simply too provocative.... knowing
the outcome may (and probably does) reduce
the power of the article for me. I'm finding it
very frustrating to read them ... how about everyone else? Is no one's blood pressure up?
RSVP.

d. *The use of "We"-specification*

T5.21 I think we all need to sit down with ourselves
and seriously be honest with ourselves and ask,
Is this the kind of world we want to live in? I
think the answer is no....

e. *The use of "You"-specification*

T3.20 "Leadership" is a funny word with which to head
this article ... it's rather ambiguous, don't'cha
think?

T5.26 Well, I believe that this bomb thing was nothing
more than a tactic to get the black protestors out
of the store—perhaps the store manager himself
called in the bomb threat. What do you think?

This kind of "you-address" clearly differs from the "you" of
direct address to a named writer, as in T4.21, entitled "reply2sammy":
I agree with your feelings ... Would you not also be reducing
yourself to their level.... or 4.44: Dear Donna, I too think that
these are driving me nuts. I agree with everything you say. First
of all....

One example in the Transparent conference uses line spacing to set up an ambiguous situation of address. That is, the writer may intend the closing questions to use global "you" to address all readers or writers, but the passage begins with specific address to two preceding writers:

> "I have just now read the two responses which came before mine. . . . Come on guys, were you just looking for short articles to which you could respond briefly? Don't you get it at all??? Do you have feelings?????

f. *expostulation*

> T3.03   who the hell wrote this thing? Gee, the way to solve. . . .

g. *aside (usually linked to a specific student)*

> T2.18   . . . their innate "rightness" [does that make sense?]
> T4.19   I agree that the subject matter is so provocative that it is difficult to be analytical . . . still I kind of enjoy trying to read between the lines [wonder if I'm accurate?]

One of the reasons we were so intrigued by how the students used rhetorical questions was that they so clearly signaled affect and elicited emulation, the term we have been using for repetition or imitation of discourse patternings. In "Indexicality and Socialization," Elinor Ochs notes that phonological and morphological structures index sociocultural information, in that they "are widely used to key speakers' social status, role, affect, and epistemological perspective. Text structures such as repetition, reformulation, code switching, and various sequential units are also linguistic resources for indexing such local contextual dimensions" (Ochs 1990:293). Her examples, from Japanese particles, show among other things, how speech acts themselves help to constitute speech activities (295). Drawing from case marking in Samoan care-giver routines, she shows the importance of elicited imitation routines: they are explicit and provide "a high degree of scaffolding for the novice"(290). Just as titles in the conference discourse could play a dual role, by conflating both gist and the hint of affect in the writing to come, rhetorical questions had a doubled function. They presented affect as well as information; that is, they presented both propositional content and a way in which propositional content could be delivered, with relation to the situation and the context that the computer conference embodied.

In his study "Contextualization and Understanding," John Gumperz (1992:229) reviews how utterances are interpreted. The "situated interpretation of any utterance is always a matter of inferences made within the context of an interactive exchange." The writings in the computer conferences could be considered as interactive exchange; what the students had to do was draw inferences in order to interpret the newspaper prompts and the writings of their classmates, in the medium of asynchronous electronic discourse. Conference discourse exploits the text and its multiple contextualization, since it can only suggest the prosody and paralinguistic signs of speech, in order to highlight, foreground, or make salient. This is not to say that electronic discourse is not social; it is the reverse. The student writers, in the absence of certain overt features of face-to-face conversation or dialogue, move to the dialogic and manipulate multiple aspects of voice in written text. They chime into each others' writing at the boundaries and frames, to the foregrounded and highlighted single words or phrases and genre or script cues, because in a face-to-face conversation, this is where they would overlap, take turns, interrupt, or bid for the floor.

What our students had in place of perception of phonemes and morphemes was the perception of text, onto which they mapped their knowledge of both text and conversation repertoires. The TTR shifts helped us to see what the writers had foregrounded. They read titles for greetings and for clues that would help them create situated interpretations, draw inferences, make choices keyed to their understanding of context. They engaged in these activities, we think, in their effort to make sense out of their context. They expected, and Gumperz claims that contextualization may raise such expectations, that their effort would "yield predictions about possible outcomes of an exchange, about suitable topics, and about the quality of interpersonal relations" (233).

Gumperz presents a list of major cues for contextualization in spoken discourse. The computer conferences were written, not spoken, though laden with conversationlike conventions. Instead of phrase-final cues, the student writers used phrases, punctuation, and capitalization. To substitute for interphrasal transitions such as pauses, students drew on repetition, which they used again in place of intraphrasal cues such as accent. Here we suspect that the lexical repetition in the conference substituting for intraphrasal cues was, we think, the repetition of charged or loaded adjectives and the *it*-clauses used to express emotive response.

Students presented themselves as authorities over text and authorities in and as themselves, by shifting registers reflecting and projecting information and involvement, and by emulating each others' shifts. They emulated strategies and propositions, they imitated ways to signal affect with strategies ranging from adverbial clauses to verb choices to rhetorical questions. Persistently, even stubbornly, even as they imitated each others' behaviors in their kaleidoscope of written exchanges, they maintained their own patterns of expression, their own preferences for sharing their thoughts and feelings. They were engaged with the text they found, the texts they created, the act of textualization they became. They were using language in a medium that was new to them for a common task, to respond to language used in a time before most of them had been born.

As an illustration of the power of rhetorical questions and the multiple layers of repetition and emulation, we reprint Calla's writings as an Appendix (D2). Writing in the Transparent conference, Calla played the titling game on occasion, responded directly and indirectly to classmates on both campuses, shifted register and rhetorical strategy, and maintained her own voice, her idiolect, in the act of contextualization.

9:// Conclusion

In this study, we have examined a corpus of interactive mainframe conference discourse, finding it to combine features of both the written text that it is and the oral text that it reads like. Baldwin (1996) calls this variety of English "textual conversation." Ferrara, Brunner, and Whittemore (1991) label it "Interactive Written Discourse." This written text has the immediacy characteristic of speech and the permanence characteristic of writing. Its written features seem to be most like texts in the genre of official letters (Biber 1988). Because of the situationally cued style shifts that its writers replicated over time and situation in three differently situated electronic conferences, we have claimed that it is apparently an emergent register. In electronic discourse, we find student writers drawing on their own idiolectal preferences from their repertoires of oral and written discourse strategies. Both the concept and the term of idiolect have implications for the study of writing, particularly the interactive writing of electronic text.

Idiolect can be distinguished from two related terms, dialect and register, in several ways. Introductory texts in linguistics, such as that by Fromkin and Rodman, define *idiolect* in this way: "The unique characteristics of the language of an individual speaker are referred to as the speaker's idiolect" (1993:276). *Dialect* is usually taken to mean a set of features keyed to regional or social contexts that characterize the ways members of a particular speech community use language. *Register* is an even more slippery term used to refer to how context evokes a "special verbal style" that is adopted in and particularized to specific social situations. A common example of register is a simplified version of language such as baby

157

talk, teacher talk, or foreigner talk (see Ochs 1992:335, Ferguson 1994). Scholars have studied the register of professions such as sportswriters and coaches, and a wide range of other socially-cued language varieties (see the articles in Biber and Finegan 1994). The particular style may include variation from the speaker's norm on any level of language, and may even be characterized as a genre in and for itself, such as prayer (see Swales 1990). The analysis of successive chunks of text and the ways the writers vary their amount of repetition can serve as a signpost to looking at the range and function of variation within the student writers' performances.

Like speakers, writers choose to signal something with a discourse shift at morphological, syntactic, lexical, or rhetorical levels, and that "something" triggers increased or lowered repetition in successive chunks of a particular writing. For example, these instances of "reported" speech or writing will trigger a discernible change in the TTRs for lexical variation: verbatim quotation of single word; quotation of phrase; quotation of clause, sentence, or passage; paraphrase; and summary.

What TTR can identify, among other things, is the pervasiveness and the persistence of a writer's habits. Literary critics speak of a writer's "style"; rhetoricians of a speaker's or writer's "voice" (Yancey 1994). While these terms are certainly not describing the same phenomena, they overlap, and they share that overlap with "idiolect" and possibly with "register." We have not presumed to ascribe "style" in the sense of artistically created literature to these first-draft chunks of rapid-draft electronic discourse composed extemporaneously at the keyboard, nor would we claim that we isolate all aspects of a writer's "voice." What we have reconstructed, described, and analyzed is written text that shares many features with conversation, including its interactivity and its shifts of styles in the ordinary sense. For this reason, when analyzing electronic discourse, we claim that it is appropriate to use the term *idiolect*.

Type-token ratio highlights lexical repetition in a writer's idiolect, the unique characteristics of the writer who is composing extemporaneously and rapidly at a keyboard in order to save and send a statement or message to other members of an electric conference. In this study, we have used TTR as an initial way to delineate and isolate comparable segments of text within the corpus, finding these segments, or chunks, to match fairly well with student-generated boundaries within the narratives they wrote. Hand-tagging the corpus for grammatical features allowed us to identify how features in use might indicate different boundaries of the social situation that the electronic conference imposed upon its members and which boundaries they stretched in different ways, depending on their own purposes for creating meaning and interaction in the situation as they perceived it.

Going across local boundaries

By changing the audience for the three conferences, we changed setting in the sense of social spaces for their participants. The first conference (Stand Alone) took place separately on each campus. Though students on each campus knew a class on the other campus was also engaged in the same conference, they did not see each others' writing. The second conference (Exchange) took place separately on each campus, but at their close, the conferences were exchanged, and students read and responded to the conference from the other campus. The third conference was Transparent. It was mounted on the mainframe on the Charlotte campus, which was linked to the Greensboro mainframe by DECNET, so that students on both campuses could access the conference simultaneously. From the students' perspective they were writing in the same conference. Geographical distance was not a factor.

To see how students in the Transparent conference were engaged in interaction with each other's writing, for example, we first examined if and how student writers signaled direct or indirect address across the mental constructs of class sections on one or both campuses. These constructs had their basis in reality, yet students chose to cross the boundary of "our group." A charting of direct and indirect address showed that just over 25 percent (twelve of the forty-six entries in topic 2) crossed class section and campus boundaries by directing one or more parts of their postings to specific people or named postings.

In electronic discourse, as well as in other kinds of discourse, direct address is one way of indicating referentiality. In the Transparent conference of 1991, the titling game (in which students engaged in word play with each others' titles) set the stage for direct address. This game provided a greeting formula, sanctioning students from any class section or campus to address the writer of a particular posting by the first name, which had been used in the title. Using first names offered writers who did not know each other some sort of social balance.

Indirect address in electronic conference discourse was more common than direct, particularly as students chimed in to different subtopics, themes, metaphors, or lexical items, sustaining argument and presenting polite forms of agreement and disagreement. Repetition and allo-repetition on multiple levels were evidently the unmarked, expected ways that writers signaled a continuum of reactions to each other's writings. The continuum ranged from tolerance to enthusiastic support: repetition functioned as a means to signal consent and adherence to the views of other student writers. Disagreement or challenge was marked, often literally with punctuation marks, and frequently by some sort of rhetorical staging or scaffolding.

The student writers in all three of the Sit-Ins conferences conventionally marked disagreement in two ways. They chimed in to what they perceived as a topical theme, either by directly repeating a word or a phrase from a preceding argument—usually with quotation marks or an introductory phrase—or with synonyms, morphological extension, or paraphrase before presenting a "different," and hence disagreeing, viewpoint. Disagreement was usually handled indirectly. When disagreement was direct, students usually included an act of apology and elaborated their rationale. Especially strong alignment was also marked: it was usually indicated by repetition followed by elaboration, heightening the effect. When alignment was combined with a direct address to a specific writer or a larger, indeterminate audience of peers, students prefaced their alignment either with explanation of personal values or with praise and approbation for the writer whose posting they had chosen. The topical theme—we might call it an "issue" or a "trope" or "what is being written about"—chosen from a preceding posting for such repetition was typically located in either the topic or the focus position at the sentence level. Here is where the issue of idiolect comes into play, using their own preferred ways of writing, sustained those patterns throughout their participation in the conference. As Pinker comments about conversation in *The Language Instinct*:

When a series of facts comes in succession, as in a dialogue
or text, the language must be structured so that the listener can
place each fact into an existing framework. Thus information
about the old, the given, the understood, the topic, should go
early in the sentence, usually as the subject, and information
about the new, the focus, the comment, should go at the end.
(Pinker 1994: 227)

Conference discourse in our corpus was neither oral conversation nor, usually, planned and edited exposition. Instead, with its
heavy contextualization and its extemporaneous keyboard composition, it was more like a multiparty conversation among strangers
who are becoming acquaintances. In the absence of the social cues
provided in face-to-face settings, student writers exploited patterns
habitual in their own idiolects to signal a range of speech acts, and
devised text-based social signals. One student might consistently
use the topic-focus pattern for recounting events and reverse it for
emphasis; another might try to present a distancing from events
with *it*-clauses; a third might use cleft sentences to place the "new"
information in the "given" position to contextualize the recount of
a strong memory or powerful emotion. Looking at patternings such
as these helps the reader reconstruct the interactivity among students during the time they participated in the conference.

Reading the text after the conference

There are problems in "reading" the transcript of a conference once
one is outside it, because reading in a linear and sequential way, one
page or one response after another, does not adequately replicate
the students' comment that the conference "feels interactive." While
a student was "in" the conference, reading and writing, the person
was interactive with texts, and with constructs of the texts' writers,
as well as of an audience that could read any reply the student left
behind in writing. The student could and apparently did go in any
direction: up and down when reading consecutive postings within a
topic, sideways or laterally to a new topic, and then up and down
again. The student could carry gists interwoven with gists from one
topic to another, one posting to another. This illusory movement

took place in space and time upon the screen in nested hierarchies, which the student networked or webs in his or her mind, probably using different spaces and times.

As well as texts, there were writers to address, all "there," all attainable. The reader/writer in the Sit-Ins conferences suspended the normal linear conventions of text while using them for navigation and construction with the texts and the other writers as partners. This partnership could be minimal or very strong. Repetition and emulation showed the movement and the amount of partnering that was going on by displaying how writers chimed in to each others' comments. Once the conference is over, however, it is an artifact—and it is "over." It is finished. And it is "read" differently: topics become chapters, even in print-out. Students forgot how to read across to find their entries. When one group was presented with the print-out of the full conference, they were momentarily puzzled until they could spread it out across space and re-created the sense of connection they had when they were part of the conference. Reading the artifact after the fact demands a topical orientation which is not always sequential and can be thematic across time and space.

Students generated their own topics within the overall issues of language use in the newspaper articles written originally as the Sit-Ins occurred. These, surfacing in topic after topic, conference upon conference, could include:

- personal response to the events and the racism those events presented;
- personal response to the media of the period as reflected in what the reporter or the newspapers sanctioned as reportage;
- personal response to the period itself and to racism in general as triggered by a closer examination of specific uses of language in the newspaper reports, as prompted by the instructors;
- personal response to the writings by peers in the conference as they presented their personal ideas, opinions, interpretations, and feelings triggered by the events, the writing, and the language used in the newspaper stories;
- personal response to the student's own feelings, interpretations, ideas, and opinions on all and any of the above, including events from the student's own personal history and the

way that students saw the general history of "my culture, my time, and place."

Their personal responses could take any of several forms, such as ventilating, validating, claiming, justifying, disclosing, narrating, challenging, agreeing, dissenting, asking, replying, explaining, and a host of other language acts, which they used daily in conversation and probably rather frequently in writing. The situation in which the students found themselves—the asynchronous multiparty interactive electronic conference—was new to them. They drew on what they knew already, from what Becker (1995) calls a "lifetime of texts."

A notion of virtual community

The collection of individual student writings, the postconference artifact of writers working in the conference, conveyed the students' notions of group or community. The students began as groups in university classes; the conferences conferred community upon them. However, once in the conferences, a sense of their own community, based on shared task, shared purpose, and the evolvement of shared norms, arose. They created additional meanings by presenting replicated, hence sanctioned, interactions, which were contiguous throughout the text and across the text: the interactions certainly felt as though they were both paradigmatic and syntagmatic. People wanted their language contact to mean something. They wanted the postings to "make sense" and they wanted to exploit the resources they brought to the conference, resources drawn from their previous educational socialization with print literacy and also from their lifetime of conversation, in order to create additional or new meaning.

The Titling Game played by students throughout the Transparent conference involved students in play with each other, but did not present the only affective cues for the reader to use in selecting a student text as the entryway into the conference. This meant that students first entering the conference could have been equally attracted by the title of the newspaper text and the number of postings it had already gathered from readers at one or both campuses rather than by the titles of specific postings. This is the phenomenon of the crowded kitchen at the successful party; students tended to gather at the Notes-Topics that have active participation, the activity being indicated by the Topics list when they enter the conference. The titling game served as a greeting mechanism, because to play it, the student writer had to self-name, which presented some social cues to other readers and may have promoted direct address.

If some sort of habitual performance and community enculturation was at work, did it occur within a single topic or might it be initiated within a single conference, reinforced by the writer's finding similar reinforcements and indexicality in the other conferences visited? This is, in effect, a language contact issue, and while titles alone—any more than any other "greeting"—cannot carry the whole load, we did look, as one would in studies of conversational routines, scripts, and frames, at the openings of this contact situation to discern patterns. Sometimes these patterns became formulas; on occasion, the formulas suggested gender-based distinctions.

The power of formula held for students on both campuses, whether they were writing in isolated or linked conferences: once a student, male or female, decided to write headlinelike titles, join in the Titling Game, present emotive signals, or note the number of replies written, that student maintained her or his pattern. Almost half of the males on both campuses devised single-word titles like Fred's. That word was what Fred felt to be the message-bearing word, and he retrieved it from the title of the newspaper story to which he was appending a posting—for example, "Bombscare." When males developed two- or three-word titling patterns, they often alternated them with another formula, such as the ones created by Karl. Even within such brief titles, he included direct address to other members of the temporary conference community by appending the number of the posting as well as the name of the writer or writing being addressed: *Go Masterson! 3.10* [to a student writer on his campus]; *Positivity 4.09* [directed to a titled writing from the other campus]; *Eloquence Jaye* [to a student writer on his own campus].

A final comment

Formulas have a purpose: the oral poet and the student writer both have them at their disposal. Fleischman reminds us that epic formulas are "a mechanism essential to the process of composition-in-performance as well to the reception and retention of material in primary oral epics. They are also culturally essential references to the tradition they encapsulate and transmit" (1990:21) Watkins notes that formulas "tend to make reference to culturally significant features or phenomena—'something that matters'"(Watkins 1989:793).

Electronic discourse, like any other use of language performed by people in interaction for the purpose of making or sharing meaning, is replete with formula: the repetition of words and phrases, the replication of patterns in titling, the emulation of strategies such as rhetorical questions. Individuals presented their own styles and maintained them across topic. As their stance shifted, so did their variation. As they established and guarded their own territories, legitimating themselves to speak on controversial and sensitive issues with each other, they presented their own individual performances, replicating their own stylistic preferences with discourse signatures keyed to their individual repetition and variation. Electronic discourse, as a variety of language, a "writing talking," is as complex, as varied, and as individual as the people who engage in its exchange.

Appendices

This section presents three types of appendices. Type 1, which includes Appendices A, B and C, consists of appendices which amplify or tabulate additional information addressed in specific chapters. Appendix A expands table 1.3 in chapter 1, by adding information about public and private verbs and root, or deontic, modality. Appendix B displays interaction among public and private verbs, intensifiers, downtoners and negation for all writers of 150 or more word entries in Notes-Topic 2 of the Transparent conference. Appendix C analyzes direct and indirect address and narrative components for all writings on the day which was the first peak of interaction among writers from both campuses involved with the Transparent conference.

Type 2, which includes Appendices D.1–D.6, presents a series of examples of techniques used in this study. Appendix D includes the online version of a single conference writing by "Calla", the text of all of Calla's electronic discourse, followed by excerpts from the word-level tagging, the concordance, and the index to Calla's single conference writing, and a graph of the type-token ratio for successive 50-word chunks of that writing. Similar tagging, concordancing, indexing and graphing was carried out for every writing that was 150 or more words in length (see tables in Chapter 1 for additional details about the corpus).

Type 3 includes Appendices E.1–E.2. Appendix E.1 lists tagging codes for linguistic features tagged in corpus items. Appendix E.2 presents a comparison of frequencies for tagged features in the same Notes-Topic across two different conference situations. (The Stand Alone conference involved writers from the same campus;

the Transparent conference involved writers from two campuses). We include these appendices for the convenience of other analysts of usage features in written asynchronous electronic communication.

Appendix A. Modality, narrative, and TTR

This table illustrates features of epistemic and root modality in a segment which correlates onset/orientation, narrative and coda with (b) TTR-segments. See Chapter 1 for a brief discussion of how narrative and TTR segments correlate in this writing; here, we expand that figure to show modality including root modality (volition, permission, obligation) and epistemic (degrees of certainty and possibility) in modal verbs

Segment		Text	Modality
Coda-3	1	-< shandie's thoughts >-	
Orientation	2	*i thought that the article was sympathetic for the time in which it was //	*mental act*
			private verb
	3	written. #i don't think that they gave enough information about the //	*negative, private verb*
	4	facts as they were but then again,i don't think it would be possible //	*downtoner, negative, private verb, conditional + possessive*
	5	seeing as how everyone views things differently.	
		#the issues of civil //	*impersonal + private verb*
Narr-1	6	*rights are interesting to me yet i really don't understand why the //	*intensifier, negative, private verb*
	7	black population was treated this way to begin with. #i know this is //	*private verb*
	8	probably because i did not grow up in this span of time and i have //	*downtoner, negative*
	9	always gone to desegregated schools.	
		#it makes me feel strange to think//	*temporal adverb, private verb, extraposition + adjective*
Narr-2	10	*about not having gone to school with all different races. #i think it //	*negative*
	11	has helped me get a better outlook on different cultures and to become //	
	12	a more well-rounded person. #i would like to think that i would not //	**negative, modals: volition**
	13	have treated the afro-americans this way if i had been alive back then //	*if-*
(Eval)			
Coda-1	14	*but i cannot honestly say that because i don't know what it was like//	*but, negative + modals, public verb, private verb*
Orientation	15	#the article itself surprises me by being sympathetic at a time when no /	
	16	one of the white population wanted to have anything to do with civil //	*[negative+] indefinite subject of infinitive*
HI TTR	17	rights. #it really surprised me to read the word "orderly" describing //	*extraposition, private verb*
Narr3	18	*the blacks [sic] students as they were leaving the store. #the wording used	*temporal as*
	19	makes the white people look worse mannered than the black students. #i	*worse than*
LO TTR	20	think the writer of this article deserves great credit for his her	*private verb*
Coda-2	21	choice of words. #the style chosen is in direct conflict with the actual	
	22	*tumultous times of the 60's civil rights movement. //	

Appendix B. Interaction: Downtoners and Intensifiers by public and private verbs for all TTR-writers—Transparent Topic 2

Entry Number	Campus/Class	Chunk 1	Chunk 2	Chunk 3	Chunk 4	Chunk 5	Chunk 6
202	UNCC Sec. 2	70 really private: find	84 private: believe	74	82 only public: suggest	80 public: suggest *could be3*	86 a lot
203	UNCC Sec. 1	78 public: agree *cannot agree*	78 public: say public: feels private: see	80 public: agree			
204	UNCC Sec. 1	76 *may trace*	84 *can be*	84 only IF *can't take3 may protect3*	?		
207	UNCC Sec. 1	70 private: felt private: remember	90 only private: find private: hope *could relate?3*	86 really *can't work?3*	?		
208	UNCC Sec. 1	78 private: meant	86 just	80 only private: noticed	84 just only IF	? public: explained private: know/neg	
209	UNCC Sec. 2	78	80 private: mean	80	72 just private: feel	— private: felt	

Appendix B. *(continued)*

Entry Number	Campus/Class	Chunk 1	Chunk 2	Chunk 3	Chunk 4	Chunk 5	Chunk 6
210	UNCC Sec. 1	78 just *couldNstopX*	80 prv:noticed prv:remember	78 public:agree,a gree prv: remember	~		
216	UNCC Sec. 2	82	72	86 private: think *could beX3*	82 IF private: think	~	
217	UNCG	76 private: think-neg private: think-neg private: thought	84 really private: feel private: know private: under-stand-neg	74 IF private: think private: think	90 really public: say private: know *cannot say*	82	~ private: think
218	UNCG	76 public: agree	76	72 private: think	82	78	70 private: think private: think
220	UNCC Sec. 1	70 IF *can't tell*	74 private: suppose	76 private: feels	~ only		

Appendix B. *(continued)*

Entry Number	Campus/Class	Chunk 1	Chunk 2	Chunk 3	Chunk 4	Chunk 5	Chunk 6
229	UNCC Sec. 1	68 IF	80 private: know private: mean	78 just private: think-neg	82 private: think-neg	76 private: feel private: think *can find out*	~ private: think *could have been?* *could have shown?*
230	UNCG	86 public: agree	80	80 only private: think	~ just		
231	UNCG	86 only	68 *could be saved?* *could N /be served]?*	86 only IF	~ IF private: think *could exist?*		
232	UNCG	82 public: agree	78 private: feels *could get?*	80 private: thought *might beX*	~ private: think		
234	UNCG	74 just private: think-neg private: canNbelieve *could have been3X*	76 IF private: think *might have*	80 private: feel	72	74 a lot private: notice	~ IF

Appendix B. *(continued)*

Entry Number	Campus/Class	Chunk 1	Chunk 2	Chunk 3	Chunk 4	Chunk 5	Chunk 6
239	UNCC Sec. 2	76 only *could tell*	78 a lot IF	88 private: imagine *cld/Nimagine*	~		
244	UNCC Sec. 1	80 private: felt private: seen	80 IF	68	~ *just*		
246	UNCC Sec. 1	80 really private: remember	78 only IF	84 *can call3*	~ private: think		
249	UNCC Sec. 1	84 public: believe	80	74 private: found private: found	~ private: know- ques		

Notes:

Numbers = Type-token ratio for that segment

~ = Indicates a segment that had fewer than 50 words (but did have 25 or more words); did not calculate TTR for these segments

shading = A segment with negation

Appendix C. October 24: First peak of interaction, all 3 classes in the transparent conference

Direct and Indirect Address in Titles and Narratives for October 24

This table displays the appearance of cues indicating direct or indirect address in titles and in successive narrachunks within all writings on a single day of the Transparent Conference. This day was the first peak of interaction for the conference that involved students from both campuses (UNC-Greensboro and UNC-Charlotte) and from both classes at UNC-Charlotte.

Referential cues to direct/indirect address:
1 names a specific person by first or last name or userid
2 names a specific writing
3 presents a cue that writing is in context of previous writing by self /others
4 uses a pronoun, e.g., you, we, our class...
5 presents other audience-cueing, "broadcast" to all

Narrative Components
O=onset, initial frame
N=narrative; ordered sequentially with keyword
C=Coda for narrative
T=Title ('real' coda:last line written, first line read)

Student identification: (Students numbered sequentially, in the order of their responses)
Ca=Charlotte class section 1   Cb=Charlotte class section 2   G =Greensboro class

October 24: First Peak of Interaction, All 3 Classes

Student	Entry No.	Specific Cues	Narrative Structures
Ca-1	220	3: I, too, was intrigued by	O reflexive writing (refers to 203: specific worduse]
			N1 evaluation of newspaper article
		1: I'm sorry that INITIALS is so turned off	N2 student claim, refers to 2.19 on Christianity
			N3 rationale for N2
			C negative evaluation of events cited in article, summary of N3

Appendix C. *(continued)*

G-1	221		T cues issues discussed:Christianity and Racism O evaluates article'seffect N1 "nonchalant" use of language, as being C writer's self-protection T cues writer by initials and focus: XX's Analysis
G-1	424	3: **Here again,** I noticed	O reflexive [< refers to 221, "nonchalant"] N1 emotions keyed to white perspective, C hence biased T cues writer by initial, focus: X's Analysis
G-2	805	2: in agreement with the **first reply** here	O reference to 801 N1 subjectivism in articles of the period N2 rationale behind N1 C evaluates purpose of article T cues writer by first name and number: X's 3d reply
G-2	1104	3: **I also find** this article to be more 3: **Like the other** responses 2: In answer **to Rambling's question**	O reference to the 3 preceding responses N1 queries regarding facts in article N2 information about journalistic styles 'requested' in 1103 C projection and evaluation of journalistic styles T cues writer by first name and number: X's 4th reply
G-3	425	5: **Well,**	O lack of change in the South today N1 reference to "fire-setting" (402, 404-5, 408, 414,422) N2 bias C addresses all readers in conference
G-4	222	4: **Thanks** for **your time**...look forward to more of your responses	T cues writer by first name, affect, [joke?]: X tries to think O historical note N1 sit-ins, rights of people at that time N2 clarifies N1 C self-assessment

Appendix C. *(continued)*

G-4	314	5: [question] I am somewhat confused, does anybody know ...	T cues writer by first name and number: X's 2nd reply
G-4	426	5: [poses question] I would like to know where... 4: Before you all write	O question: facts reported in article N1 evaluates style of article's close C pun on N1, projection regarding reporter T cues writer by first name and number: X's 2nd reply O question: facts reported in article N1 continues questions, some irony? N2 new questions, irony surfaced "could have just thought" C summary which answers both sets of questions T cues writer by first name and number: X's 3rd reply
Cb-2	223		O It-that summary regarding emotions in 60s N1 student protest in 60s, compared with now C glad not victim as in the 60s T [blank]
Cb-2	224		O It-that deplores N1 "in 60s" N2 expands Conclusion from 223 C projection of self to 60s T first word in newspaper headline: Aid
Cb-3	427	5: Give me a break!	O personal reaction N1 discrimination as appalling N2 as Northerner, reviews South, with examples e.g., friend's father, KKK C evaluation, disgust (Colloquial invitation for assent, echo, solidarity) T cues writer
Cb-4	428		O evaluates article N1 expands O, echoes phrase of 427 N2 conflates KKK and businessmen

Appendix C. *(continued)*

Cb-3	904	5: Just give it a rest.	C evaluation, disgust: (colloquial signal, echo 427) T [blank]
Cb-2	429	5:I would like to know	O evaluation of all articles N1 series of rhetorical questions regarding reacism C indirect contradiction to C of 903 T cues writer,issue: racist reply XX
			O rhetorical question N1 personal reaction to setting coat on fire (425) N2 on 5th day, number of people involved in fire N3 white language used to abuse C summary of protest, allocates blame T cues C, allocates blame: 'white'
Cb-4	1008		O personal reaction to all articles in conference N1 expands O C restates reaction T cues writer and number: X3
Cb-2	511	5:I wonder who 3: whites were still being abusive	O rhetorical question N1 evaluates events in the series of questions, answers N2 echoes own 429 C rhetorical question T variant, first word in title, newspaper article but not title

Appendix D1. Sample analysis: One of Calla's entries, Transparent Conference

1. SAMPLE ENTRY FROM THE CONFERENCE

```
===================================================================
Note 11.3        Sit Down Movement Began Last Week        3 of 7
STEFFI::[CALLA]                               22 lines  21-OCT-1991 17:55
            -< rambling >-
-------------------------------------------------------------------
```

I find this article to be quite sympathetic with the cause of the
students. It is obvious from the word choice of the author that he
belives that the students are correct in what they are trying to do,
and that he believes the KKK and the hecklers are the ones presenting
the problems (which in my opinion, as most will agree, was indeed the
problem). The newspaper, like most media services, makes certain their
opinion is clearly presented throughout its articles, thus the reporter
does not make any attempt to present both sides of the situation. He
wants the reader to feel sympathy with the students who are being
subjected to this type of treatment while merely trying to be treated
as equal citizens.

However, in many places, he seems to use constructions and which are
hard to follow or understand in the context within which they are used.
This creates a story which is in some places hard to understand. The
author also seems to include unnecessary pieces of information and
leave out things which would be useful to know (such as the elusive
reasons why the arrests were made). One is left wondering why the
author or editor made these choices. But the main problem I keep
running into throughout these articles is there choppiness. Each
sentence is a new paragraph which may or may not have anything to do
with the rest of the story. Why?

Appendix D2. Calla's writings in the transparent conference

5.01 -< gut reaction >-

My gut reaction to this story is how horrible it must have been to those students sitting at the lunch counter. All they were trying to do is to demand the very rights assured to them by the constitution in a peaceful, non-violent manner, and they are met with such horrible violence directed at them.

No, this reaction has nothing to do with what we are supposed to be discussing here, but I couldn't leave the lab without commenting on my feelings. More to come later.

Calla

11.03 -< rambling >-

I find this article to be quite sympathetic with the cause of the students. It is obvious from the word choice of the author that he belives that the students are correct in what they are trying to do, and that he believes the KKK and the hecklers are the ones presenting the problems (which in my opinion, as most will agree, was indeed the problem). The newspaper, like most media services, makes certain their opinion is clearly presented throughout its articles, thus the reporter does not make any attempt to present both sides of the situation.

He wants the reader to feel sympathy with the students who are being subjected to this type of treatment while merely trying to be treated as equal citizens. However, in many places, he seems to use constructions which are hard to follow or understand in the context within which they are used. This creates a story which is in some places hard to understand. The author also seems to include unnecessary pieces of information and leave out things which would be useful to know (such as the elusive reasons why the arrests were made). One is left wondering why the author or editor made these choices. But the main problem I keep running into throughout these articles is there choppiness. Each sentence is a new paragraph which may or may not have anything to do with the rest of the story. Why?

3.13 -< Calla's reply >-

As others have written this article reads like an editorial. It has a thesis and cites only the points and "facts" for the mere purpose of proving this thesis. It is a thesis that makes it quite clear which side of the sit-ins the author agrees with, despite the fact that he never explicitly states his purpose for writing. The author belives that the proper way of handling things would be through negotiation with the business leaders. I agree with Terri who wrote "where was this man, on the moon?" Anyone who has any idea of what was actually going on in the world knows that the protestors would have gotten nowhere following the "proper channels." These channels were designed specifically to hold the minorities back and keep the society unequal. How could they have gotten any where within these channels?

The author's tone causeses me to wonder if he is a store owner himself whose business is being hurt by the sit in he is so obviously against. His suggestion of more "separate but equal" facilities in WoolWorth is also offensive. Doesn't he have any idea what the people involved in the sit-ins were after? Maybe following his line of thought each of his suggestions would have worked, we could have black leaders pettitioning the store owners for more black facilities, but that is not what the protests

Appendix D2. Calla's writings in the transparent conference *(continued)*

were about. This dude needs to get more than just a summer home in reality. The author systematically and repeatedly downplays the sit-ins, and along with attempting to make them seem unnecessary. These points along with his suggestion to store owners to have the protestors arrested as trespassers reveal his true feelings about the situation, but these are not something he tries to hide, rather he comes off looking like he is quite proud of his beliefs. He reminds me just a little too much of the guy I saw today in a film about the attempts to desegregate the buses of Montgomery, Al, who tried to prove that desegregation was against the Bible. It all seems to be just a little too unbelievable (not that these things happened, but that people actually belived this stuff, and that many continue to belive it today. It's really quite sad.) This author seems to be saying that the blacks should be happy to have what they have and therefore should "stay in their place," thereby remaining second class citizens and subordinate to the whites.

As for the violence this author seems to fear, it was not the blacks who used violence. Rather, it was the close minded, racist whites that felt the need to add violence to the situation. The blacks were merely non-violently and passively protesting the segregation, and demanding their God given, and Constitutionally guaranteed, right to equality.

4.22 -< Calla's reply >-

In response to why the addresses are given for the men arrested (questions raised by Answer1a, and Connolly), they are generally used for the purpose of identification, just in case there are other men running around out there with the same name. I do agree with the thoughts that these men probably were quite proud of the fact that they were arrested, feeling that they had made a stand. But, in my opinion, this is merely the product of their own twisted minds, and that the paper probably had no intention of saying "look ya'll, these men did what they should and set fire to one of them....." To feel the need to feel that I am better than someone else for any reason (much less something as stupid as skin color, gender, sexual preference,or IQ) is truly a horrible position to be in. And, to fulfill this need by setting another human being on fire is completely demented and despicable. I also am suprised at the fact that the author includes the fact that Palmer uses a burning piece of paper, usually the type of weapon used in a charge such as this is left out of the newspaper report. I agree that it was probably the author's attempt to say how stupid he felt the charges were. As for Fuller not being injured, being set on fire seems to me to be injury enough, whether he sustained any burns or not!

But, what I want to know is if the author would have given the addresses of any blacks who might have been arrested? or would he have let the confusion of persons with the same name go on? He did not give the address of Fuller, but is this out of protection of the party? or in hope that it will cause problems for someone else?

As for the quoting of the KKK Klud (or is that clod), I find it to be truly offensive. The treatment of the Klud also contrasts greatly with that of the treatment of X, the only black person to be quoted in the entire article. The KKK is depicted as being patriotic, benevolent and caring; and, yet, everyone knows that it is made up of the most closed minded, violent, and offensive people in this country. I question whether he was really there to keep violence from happening, or if he was there to create it if given the chance. Maybe Fuller was set on fire because of an order from Mr. Clod, we'll never know. As for X, the very idea of calling a person by a letter is demeaning, and the author's choice of letters is suprising.

Appendix D2. Calla's writings in the transparent conference *(continued)*

The author obviously thinks the protest is out of line as is seen in not only the fact that he quotes the KKK, but also (as noted by Bob Stevens) in the fact that the author refuses to acknowledge the blacks as being people. The naming of a human being using one single, solitary letter is offensive and demeaning. The choice of the letter "X" is interesting in the fact that it also reveals the author's viewpoint. X=wrong or incorrect, we use this letter to grade everything in sight and it generally is used to mark things out (ie: days of a calendar, etc.) when they are over. And this author selects this letter to refer to a person?!?

The author further reveals his feeling about the situation in the fact that he actually gives authority to the Clod to speak by making reference to the fact that a Clod is a Chaplain of the KKK; and yet, the author refuses to acknowledge anything at all about "X," thereby not even giving him the authority to speak for himself much less anyone else.

4.23 -< response to Candace>-

I promise to keep this one fairly short. Honest. But, I feel the need to respond to Candace's question of why the Blacks were happy when the stores closed down. The basic reason is the point you already raised, it hurt the revenues of the store. Hurting someone in the pocketbook is the most effective way to bring about social change. By forcing the stores to close down, the stores were unable to earn any profit and no store can last very long without a profit. They have too many bills to pay, and big ones at that (If you think You've got a big electric bill to pay, take a look at one for just about any retail store. They're truly astronomical!!!). A store that can't make a profit is forced to close down and leaves the owners in bankruptcy.

Once the store closes down it can be replaced with one that is more receptive to desegregation, merely because this is the only type of store that can survive a mass social movement such as this, it would be the only type with any business. No, the blacks did not reach their goal in forcing the stores to close, but they did make a step toward the ending of segregation through the closings. One small step for equality in humankind.

8.06 -< Calla's response to Peter >-

Despite the fact that the closing of the lunch counters instead of serving the students was incredibly racist, it was one of the main factors in the achieving more equal treatment. As I stated earlier in the conference, hurting the owners pocketbooks was the most effective way of reaching the sensibilities of the owners. Maybe their opinion of the blacks did not change, but they served them anyway, merely keep the counters open and make money. Besides, you can't change a lifetime of beliefs (as wrong as they were) overnight, rather you have to prove to the people over and over again that everything they had ever been told about segregation and the black race were wrong. And, in order to accomplish this feat, it would require interaction on a more equal basis, an opportunity that could only come about with desegregation.

I would like to think that desegregation will one day end all of the racism in America, but then I really have to wonder when I go out with some of my friends (friends who happen to be black) and am stared at like I am a traitor or something. The sad thing is that they also get those kind of stares and sometimes are even asked why they spend time "with that white girl." No, we're not the traitors, despite the stares. The ones giving us the hard time are. They are traitors to what they profess to believe and to the ideals that America was founded on, equality for all.

Appendix D3. Sample tagged text

2. SAMPLE TAGGED TEXT

|bT1103p01CALLA
|cT1103p01CALLA
-< rambling >-
|bT1103p02CALLA
|cT1103p02CALLA
I find VBPRES this article to be INF quite sympathetic with the cause of the
students .
It PROITEXTRA is VBBEPRES obvious from the word choice of the author that COMPTHATEXTRA he
belives VBZ that COMPTHATVB the students are VBBEPRES correct in what COMPWH they are trying VBINGPRES to do VBDOPRO INF ,
and that COMPTHATEXTRA he believes VBZ COMPTHATVB0 the KKK and the hecklers are VBBEPRES the
|bT1103p03CALLA
|cT1103p03CALLA
ones PARTPRESWHIZ presenting
the problems (which RELSENT in my opinion , as most will MODPRED agree VB , was VBBEPAST indeed the
problem) .
The newspaper , like most media services , makes VBZ certain COMPTHATADJ0 their
opinion is clearly presented PASS0 VBPRES throughout its articles . thus the reporter
does VBDOAUX VBZ not NEGANA make VB any attempt to present INF both sides of the situation . NOM
He
wants VBZ the
|bT1103p04CALLA
|cT1103p04CALLA
reader to feel INF sympathy with the students who RELWHOSUBJ are being
subjected PASS0 VBINGPRES to this type of treatment NOM while merely trying GERUND to be
treated
as equal citizens .

However , in many places , he seems VBZ VBSEEM to use INF constructions NOM and
which RELWHICHSUBJ are
hard to follow INF or understand INF in the context within which RELPIED they are used PASS0 VBPRES .

|bT1103p05CALLA
|cT1103p05CALLA
This LEXDEM creates VBZ a story which RELWHICHSUBJ is VBBEPRES in some places hard to understand INF .
The author also seems VBZ VBSEEM to include INF unnecessary pieces of information NOM
and leave out INF things which RELWHICHSUBJ would MODPRED be VB useful to know INF (such as the elusive

Appendix D3. *(continued)*

reasons why COMPWH the arrests were made PASS0 VBPAST) .
One is VBBEPRES left wondering PARTPRES why COMPWH the
author or
|bT1103p06CALLA
|cT1103p06CALLA
editor made VBPAST these choices .
But the main problem I keep running into VBINGPRES throughout
these articles is VBBEPRES there
choppiness . NOM
Each sentence is VBBEPRES a new paragraph which RELWHICHSUBJ may
MODPOSS or may MODPOSS not NEGANA have VBHAVE anything to
do INF with the rest of the story .
QUES Why ? FRAGSENT

Appendix D4.

3. SAMPLE WORD FREQUENCY FILE

```
***********  Unique Words Read =        175
***********  Total  Words Read =        323
***********  Total  Chars Read =       1595
***********  Books        Found =         6
***********  Chapters     Found =         6
***********  Paragraphs   Found =         1
[Type/token Ratio = 54·]
```

1 ?	1 hecklers	1 presenting	1 vbdoaux
2 a	1 however	2 problem	1 vbdopro
1 agree	2 i	1 problems	1 vbhave
1 also	5 in	1 proitextra	3 vbingpres
4 and	1 include	1 ques	2 vbpast
1 any	1 indeed	1 quite	3 vbpres
1 anything	12 inf	1 rambling	2 vbseem
6 are	1 information	1 reader	8 vbz
1 arrests	1 into	1 reasons	1 wants
1 article	6 is	1 relpied	1 was
2 articles	1 it	1 relsent	1 were
3 as	1 its	4 relwhichsubj	1 what
1 attempt	1 keep	1 relwhosubj	6 which
3 author	1 kkk	1 reporter	1 while
3 be	1 know	1 rest	1 who
1 being	1 leave	1 running	3 why
1 believes	1 left	2 seems	1 will
1 belives	1 lexdem	1 sentence	3 with
1 both	1 like	1 services	1 within
1 but	2 made	1 sides	1 wondering
1 cause	1 main	1 situation	1 word
1 certain	1 make	1 some	1 would
1 choice	1 makes	2 story	
1 choices	1 many	3 students	
1 choppiness	2 may	1 subjected	
1 citizens	1 media	1 such	
1 clearly	1 merely	1 sympathetic	
1 compthatadj0	2 modposs	1 sympathy	
2 compthatextra	2 modpred	3 that	
1 compthatvb	2 most	23 the	
1 compthatvb0	1 my	1 their	
3 compwh	2 negana	1 there	
1 constructions	1 new	2 these	
1 context	1 newspaper	2 they	
1 correct	5 nom	1 things	
1 creates	2 not	3 this	
2 do	1 obvious	2 throughout	
1 does	6 of	1 thus	
1 each	1 one	12 to	
1 editor	1 ones	1 treated	
1 elusive	2 opinion	1 treatment	
1 equal	3 or	2 trying	
1 feel	1 out	1 type	
1 find	1 paragraph	2 understand	
1 follow	1 partpres	1 unnecessary	
1 fragsent	1 partpreswhiz	1 use	
1 from	4 pass0	1 used	
1 gerund	1 pieces	1 useful	
2 hard	2 places	3 vb	
1 have	1 present	1 vbbepast	
4 he	1 presented	7 vbbepres	

Appendix D5.

4. SAMPLE CONCORDANCE

```
Computer Book:     C:\BYTAG\CALL1103.BYB
Style:    KWIC Concordance    { All the words }
Starting at:
Ending at:
Style Flags:      DuplctDel[Y] EmbedRef[Y] EditMark[N]
                  AbbrvBook[N] PrefHead[N]
```

```
                                     ?  (1)
T1103p06CALLA
   T1103p06:1          of the story .  QUES Why ? FRAGSENT

**********
                                     compthatadj0  (1)
T1103p03CALLA
   T1103p03:Heading       , makes VBZ certain   COMPTHATADJ0  their   opinion is clearly

                                     compthatextra  (2)
T1103p02CALLA
   T1103p02:Heading   choice of the author that  COMPTHATEXTRA  he   belives VBZ that
   T1103p02:Heading   do VBDOPRO INF ,  and that  COMPTHATEXTRA  he believes VBZ COMPTHATVB0

                                     compthatvb  (1)
T1103p02CALLA
   T1103p02:Heading       he   belives VBZ that  COMPTHATVB  the students are VBBEPRES

                                     compthatvb0  (1)
T1103p02CALLA
   T1103p02:Heading        he believes VBZ  COMPTHATVB0  the  KKK and the hecklers are

                                     compwh  (3)
T1103p02CALLA
   T1103p02:Heading    VBBEPRES correct in  what  COMPWH  they are trying VBINGPRES to
T1103p05CALLA
   T1103p05:Heading as the elusive   reasons why  COMPWH  the arrests were made PASS0
   T1103p05:Heading  left wondering PARTPRES why  COMPWH  the   author or
**********

                                     fragsent  (1)
T1103p06CALLA
   T1103p06:1          of the story .  QUES Why ? FRAGSENT
**********


                                     modposs  (2)
T1103p06CALLA
   T1103p06:1          which RELWHICHSUBJ may  MODPOSS  or may MODPOSS not NEGANA
   T1103p06:1            may  MODPOSS or may  MODPOSS  not NEGANA have VBHAVE

                                     modpred  (2)
T1103p03CALLA
   T1103p03:Heading in my opinion , as most will  MODPRED   agree VB , was VBBEPAST
T1103p05CALLA
   T1103p05:Heading    which RELWHICHSUBJ would  MODPRED  be VB  useful to know INF (
**********

                                     negana  (2)
T1103p03CALLA
   T1103p03:Heading       does VBDOAUX VBZ not  NEGANA  make VB any attempt to
T1103p06CALLA
   T1103p06:1        MODPOSS or may MODPOSS not  NEGANA  have VBHAVE anything to  do
**********

                                     proitextra  (1)
T1103p02CALLA
   T1103p02:Heading   of  the  students .  It  PROITEXTRA  is VBBEPRES obvious from the

                                     ques  (1)
T1103p06CALLA
   T1103p06:1          the rest of the story .  QUES Why ? FRAGSENT
**********
```

Appendix D6. TTR graph
single entry (11.03) by Calla

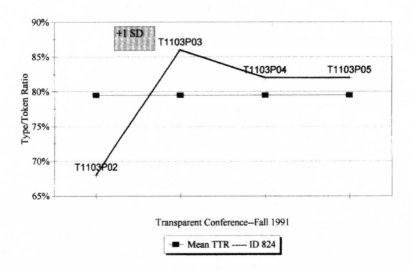

Transparent Conference--Fall 1991

Mean TTR ----- ID 824

Appendix E1.

TAGGING LIST

Note: Tagging codes are placed immediately after the word or phrase. See Biber (1988: 222-245) for his discussion of th linguistic features.

Biber #	Linguistic Feature	Tagging Codes
	absence of a feature where it can or should occur	add 0 (=zero) to the end of the code
	address titles (For titles of address (Mrs., Dr.) and honorifics (e.g. First Lady, Aunt (for example as used traditionally in the South as a title rather than as an indicator of a relative. An example would be the use of "Aunt Ruth" to refer to a neighbor rather than to refer to a member of the family).	titleadd
	entry titles (Can use after each word in the title conference or email message.)	titleconf
	Tense and Aspect Markers	See also modal verbs (# 52-54)
1	past tense	vbpast
2	perfect aspect	vbperf
3	present tense	vbpres
	verb HAVE	[vb+form] vbhave, vbhas, vbhad, vbhaving (plus contratcted forms, e.g. I've, hasn't)
	verb base form	vb
	missing verb	vb0
	3rd person, singular, present tense	vbz vbz0
	-ING verb	vbing vbingpast vbingpres vbingperf
	main verb BE	vbbe vbbepast
	regular verb	vbr
	irregular verb	vbir
	any verb (verb not marked by any of the preceding markers)	vbany

Appendix E1. *(continued)*

Biber #	Linguistic Feature	Tagging Codes
	pro-verb DO	vbdopro
	auxiliary DO	vbdoaux
	question DO	vbdoq
	main verb DO	vbdo
	split infinitives	splitinf
	split auxiliaries (he has clearly mastered the subject)	splitaux
	Place and Time Adverbials	
4	place adverbials	advplace
5	time adverbials	advtime
	Personal Pronouns	
6	first person pronouns	[pro+form] proi, prowe, prous, promy, proour, promyself, proourselves also contracted forms
7	second person pronouns	proyou, proyour, proyourself, proyourselves also contracted forms
8	third person personal pronouns	[pro+form] proshe, prohe, prothey, proher, prohim, prothem, prohis, proher, protheir, prohimself, proherself, prothemselves also contracted forms
9	pronoun IT (Tags for personal pronoun, impersonal pronoun, and IT used with extraposed sentences.)	proit, proitimp, proitextra also contracted forms
10	demonstrative pronouns (cf. with #51)	
11	indefinite pronouns (e.g., anybody, everything, someone)	proindef
12	pro-verb DO (not an auxiliary verb)	vbdopro
	auxiliary DO	vbdoaux
	question DO	vbdoq
	Questions	
	question	ques
	yes/no questions	qyes

Appendix E1. *(continued)*

Biber #	Linguistic Feature	Tagging Codes
13	WH-questions	qwhdirect qwh
	Nominal Forms	
14	nominalization (words ending in -tion, -ment, -ness, or -ity; singular and plural forms)	nom
15	gerunds	nomgerund
16	total other nouns	nounother
	Passives	
17	agentless passives	pass0
18	by-passives	passwithby
	Stative Forms	
19	BE as main verb	vbbe vbbepast
20	existential THERE	exthere (als contracted form THERE'S)
	Subordination	
21	THAT verb complements (I know that he works at the auto plant) See also #60.	compthatvb compthatvb0
22	THAT adjective complements (I'm glad that she came) See also #60.	compthatadj compthatadj0
23	WH clauses (I know what he wants)	compwh compwh0
	complements	compthatextra compthatextra0 compthat compthat0 comp comp0
24	infinitives	compinf
	Participial Forms	
25	present participial clauses	partpres
26	past participial clauses	partpast
27	past participial WHIZ deletion relatives (the report presented to the committee)	partpastwhiz
28	present participial WHIZ deletion relatives (the attitude causing this problem)	partpreswhiz

Appendix E1. *(continued)*

Biber #	Linguistic Feature	Tagging Codes
	Relatives	
29	that relative clauses on subject position	relthatsubj relthatsubj0
30	that relative clauses on object position	relthatobj relthatobj0
31	WH relative clauses in subject position	relwhosubj relwhichsubj relwhosesubj relwhosubj0 relwhichsubj0
32	WH relative clauses in object position	relwhoobj relwhichobj relwhoseobj relwhoobj0 relwhichobj0
33	pied-piping relative clauses (the manner in which he replied)	relpied
34	sentence relatives	relsent relsent0
	Adverbial Clauses	
35	causative adverbial subordinator (because)	subadvcause subadvas subadvfor subadvsince
36	concessive adverbial subordinators (although, though)	subadvaltho subadvtho
37	conditional adverbial subordinators (if, unless)	subadvif subadvunless
38	other adverbial subordinators (e.g., while, whereas, such that, as soon as)	subadvother
	Prepositional Phrases	
39	total prepositional phrases	prepos
	Adjectives and Adverbs	
40	attributive adjectives	adj
41	predicative adjectives	adjpred
42	total adverbs (other adverbs that are not included in other categories)	adv
	Lexical Specificity	

Appendix E1. *(continued)*

Biber #	Linguistic Feature	Tagging Codes
43	type/token ratio (unique words/total words)	
44	word length	
	Lexical Classes	
45	conjuncts (e.g., consequently, conversely, e.g., furthermore, moreover, nevertheless, notwithstanding, therefore, thus)	lexconjunct
46	downtoners (e.g., almost, barly, nearly, slightly, somehwat)	lexdown
47	hedges (e.g., at about, more or less, maybe)	lexhedge
48	amplifiers (e.g., absolutely, completely, extremely, totally, very)	lexamp
49	emphatics (e.g., for sure, a lot, such)	lexemph
50	discourse particles (e.g., well, now, anyhow)	lexdisc
51	demonstratives (excludes demonstrative pronouns [see #10] and THAT as a relative, complementizer, of subordinator	lexdem
	Modals	
52	possibility modals (can, may, might, could) also contractions	modposs
53	necessity modals (ought, should, must) also contractions	modnec
54	predictive modals (will, would, shall) also contractions	modpred
	Specialized Verb Classes	
55	public verbs (e.g., admit, agree, claim, deny, mention, suggst, write)	vbpub
56	private verbs (eg.g., assume, blieve, conclude, feel, find, know, learn, mean, prove, realize, remember, whow, thing, understand)	vbpriv

Appendix E1. *(continued)*

Biber #	Linguistic Feature	Tagging Codes
57	suasive verbs (e.g., ask, decide, propose, recommend, request, suggest, urge)	vbsua
58	seem/appear	vbseem/vbappear
	Reduced Forms and Dispreferred Structures	
59	contractions	contrpro[+form] contraux contrnp
60	subordinator-THAT deletion See also #21 and #22.	compthatvb0 compthatadj0
61	stranded preposition	prepstrand
62	split infinitives	splitinf
63	split auxiliaries	splitaux
	Coordination	
64	phrasal coordination	coordphr
65	independent clause coordination	coordcl
66	synthetic negation (no, neither, nor)	negsyn
67	analytic negation (not) also contracted forms	negana
	Miscellaneous	
	cleft sentences	cleftsent
	sentence fragment	fragsent
	possessives	possnp possnp0 posspro posspro0
	LIKE (for as, as if, or as though)	likeas

Appendix E2. Frequency of tagged features, same notes-topic in two conference situations

In the Stand Alone Conference students wrote exclusively to peers on their own campus. In the Transparen Conference students from two campuses wrote to each other

Linguistic Feature	Stand Alone UNCC	Transparent
past tense	95	76
perfect aspect verbs	23	17
present tense	68	62
3rd pers sing (VBZ)	38	21
ING verb past	6	6
ING verb present	1	8
ING verb perfect	0	0
BE as main verb		
BE as main verb - past	36	31
BE as main verb - present	52	54
DO as pro-verb	5	7
DO as auxiliary verb	17	14
contractions		
contraction - auxiliary	7	10
contraction - pronoun I	1	5
contraction - pronoun IT (imp)	7	2
contraction verb	2	1
possibility modals	9	17
necessity modals	5	10
predictive modals	14	19
public verbs	23	12
private verbs	65	71
suasive verbs	4	5

Appendix E2. *(continued)*

Linguistic Feature	Stand Alone UNCC	Transparent
SEEM/APPEAR	5	4
verb HAVE	9	7
Personal pronouns		
I	51	60
HE	7	10
SHE	3	3
IT	16	9
YOU	11	7
WE	10	8
THEY	27	33
pronoun IT		
pronoun IT extraposition	14	11
impersonal pronoun IT	8	11
indefinite pronouns	12	18
nominalizations	53	42
agentless passives	35	32
pass0 vbpast	22	17
pass0 vbpres	11	12
pass0vbperf	1	2
BY passives	1	2
passwithby vbpast	1	
passwithby vbpres	0	0
passwithby vbperf	0	0
existential THERE	4	7
THAT complements	14	9
THAT complements- deleted	2	6
THAT compl - extraposition	0	0
THAT compl - extra - deleted		0
THAT verb complements	29	31
THAT verb compl. - deleted	8	10
THAT adj. complements	11	4

Appendix E2. *(continued)*

Linguistic Feature	Stand Alone UNCC	Transparent
THAT adj. compl - deleted	2	1
TOTAL - THAT del. (adj&vb)	10	11
WH clauses	19	23
present participial clauses	12	12
past participial clauses	9	11
past prt. WHIZ deletions	6	6
present prt. WHIZ deletions	2	2
THAT relatives: subj. position	10	9
THAT relatives: obj. position	4	3
THAT rel.: obj. - deletion	0	0
WH relatives: subj. position	7	11
WH relatives: obj. position	0	0
WH relatives: obj. - deletion	3	1
WH relatives: pied pipes	0	0
sentence relatives	1	2
adverbs		
adv. subordinator - cause	44	40
adv. subordinator - concession	7	5
adv. subordinator - condition	8	2
adv. subordinator - other	28	21
place adverbials	10	4
time adverbials	14	14
conjuncts	10	15
downtoners	13	64
hedges	50	32
amplifiers	10	7
emphatics	29	28
discourse particles	8	5
demonstratives [lexdem]	7	10
clausal coordination	3	0

Appendix E2. *(continued)*

Linguistic Feature	Stand Alone UNCC	Transparent
synthetic negation	6	4
analytic negation	28	30
cleft sentence		1
sentence fragment	3	8
like=as	1	2
possessive 0		0
possessive np	8	7
possessive np0	1	0
possessive pronoun	2	0
possessive pro0	0	1
question (QUES - inclusive)	13	5

References

Asimov, Isaac. 1957. *The Naked Sun*. Garden City, N.Y.: Doubleday.

Baron, Naomi S. 1984. "Computer Mediated Communication as a Force in Language Change." *Visible Language* 18: 118–41.

Baldwin, Beth W. 1996. "Conversations: Computer Mediated Dialogue, Multilogue, and Learning." Ph.D. Dissertation, University of North Carolina at Greensboro. Electronic publications, http://www.missouri.edu/~rhetnet/baldwin/

Basso, Keith H. 1974. "The Ethnography of Writing." In *Explorations in the Ethnography of Speaking*, edited by Richard Bauman and Joel Scherzer, 425–32. Cambridge, England: Cambridge University Press.

Baym, Nancy K. 1995. "The Emergence of Community in Computer-Mediated Communication." In *Cybersociety: Computer-Mediated Communication and Community*, edited by Steven G. Jones, 138–63. Thousand Oaks, CA: Sage.

Becker, A. L., ed. 1995. *Beyond Translation: Essays Towards a Modern Philology*. Ann Arbor: University of Michigan Press.

Bell, Alan. 1984. "Language Style as Audience Design." *Language in Society* 13: 145–204.

———. 1995. "Language and the Media." *Annual Review of Applied Linguistics* 15: 23–31.

Benveniste, Emil. 1971. *Problems in General Linguistics*. Translated by M. E. Meek. Coral Gables: University of Miami Press.

Biber, Douglas. 1988. *Variation across Speech and Writing*. Cambridge, England: Cambridge University Press.

———. 1994. "An Analytical Framework for Register Studies." In *Sociolinguistic Perspectives on Register*, edited by Douglas Biber and Edward Finegan, 31–56. Oxford Studies in Sociolinguistics. New York: Oxford University Press.

Biber, Douglas, and Edward Finegan, eds. 1994. *Sociolinguistic Perspectives on Register.* Oxford Studies in Sociolinguistics, edited by Edward Finegan. Oxford, England: Oxford University Press.

Black, Steven D., James A. Levin, Hugh Mehan, and Clark N. Quinn. 1983. "Real and Non-real Time Interaction: Unraveling Multiple Threads of Discourse." *Discourse Processes* 6: 59–75.

Bloomfield, Leonard. 1933. *Language.* London, England: George Allen and Unwin.

Bolter, Jay. 1991. *Writing Space: The Computer, Hypertext, and the History of Writing.* Hillsdale, N.J.: Lawrence Erlbaum.

Brown, Gillian, and George Yule. 1983. *Discourse Analysis.* Cambridge, England: Cambridge University Press.

Brown, Penelope, and Stephen Levinson. 1987. *Politeness: Some Universals of Languge Usage.* Cambridge, England: Cambridge University Press.

Bybee, Joan L. 1985. *Morphology: A Study of the Relation between Meaning and Form.* Typological Studies in Language, 9. Amsterdam and Philadelphia, PA: John Benjamins.

Bybee, Joan, Revere Perkins, and William Pagliuca. 1994. *The Evolution of Grammar: Tense, Aspect and Modality in the Languages of the World.* Chicago, and London, England: University of Chicago Press.

Carpenter, Ronald H. 1990. "The Statistical Profile of Language Behavior with Machiavellian Intent or While Experiencing Caution and Avoiding Self-Incrimination." In *The Language Scientist as Expert in the Legal Setting,* edited by Robert W. Rieber and William A. Stewart, 5–18. Annals of the New York Academy of Sciences, 606.

Chafe, Wallace. 1986. "Writing in the Perspective of Speaking." In *Studying Writing: Linguistic Approaches,* edited by Charles H. Cooper and Sidney Greenbaum, 14–39. Beverly Hills, Calif.: Sage Publications.

————. 1987. "Cognitive Constraints on Information Flow." In *Coherence and Grounding in Discourse: Outcome of a Symposium, Eugene, Oregon, June 1984,* edited by Russell S. Tomlin. Typological Studies in Language, 11. Amsterdam and Philadelphia: John Benjamins.

Chafe, Wallace, and J. Danielewicz. 1987. "Properties of Spoken and Written Language." In *Comprehending Oral and Written Language,* edited by R. Horowitz and S. J. Samuels, 173–88. New York: Academic Press.

Chafe, Wallace and J. Nichols, eds. 1986. *Evidentiality: The Linguistic Encoding of Epistemology.* Norwood, NJ: Ablex.

Cheepen, Christine. 1988. *The Predictability of Informal Conversation.* London, England, and New York: Pinter Publishers.

Collot, Milena and Nancy Belmore. 1993. "Electronic Language: A New Variety of English." In *English Language Corpora: Design, Analysis and Exploitation*, edited by Jan Aarts, Pieter de Haan, and Nelleke Oostdijk, 41–55. Language and Computers: Studies in Practical Linguistics, edited by Jan Aarts and Willem Meijs, 10. Papers from the Thirteenth International Conference on English Language Research on Computerized Corpora, Nijmegen 1992. Amsterdam and Atlanta, GA: Rodopi.

Cooper, Marilyn M., and Cynthia L. Selfe. 1990. "Computer Conferences and Learning: Authority, Resistance, and Internally Persuasive Discourse." *College English* 52: 847–69.

Coulthard, Malcolm. 1994. *Advances in Written Text Analysis*. London, England, and New York: Routledge.

d'Andrade, R. G., and M. Wish. 1990. "Speech Act Theory in Quantitative Research on Interpersonal Behavior." *Discourse Processes* 8: 229–59.

Devitt, Amy J. 1989. *Standardizing Written English: Diffusion in the Case of Scotland 1520–1659*. Cambridge, England: Cambridge University Press.

Duin, Ann Hill, and Craig Hansen. 1994. "Reading and Writing on Computer Networks as Social Construction and Social Interaction." In *Literacy and Computers: The Complications of Teaching and Learning with Technology*, edited by Cynthia Selfe and Susan Hilligoss, 89–112. Research and Scholarship in Composition, 2. New York: Modern Language Association.

Dunlop, Charles and Rob Kling, eds. 1991. *Computerization and Controversy: Value Conflicts and Social Choices*. Boston, MA: Academic Press.

Duranti, Alessandro and Charles Goodwin, eds. 1992. *Rethinking Context: Language as an Interactive Phenomenon*. Cambridge, England: Cambridge University Press.

Eldred, Janet Carey, and Gail Hawisher. 1995. "Researching Electronic Networks." *Written Communication* 12: 330–59.

Faigley, Lester. 1985. "Nonacademic Writing: The Social Perspective." In *Writing in Nonacademic Settings*, edited by L. Odell and Dixie Goswami. New York: Guilford.

———. 1986. "The Problem of Topic in Texts." In *The Territory of Language: Linguistics, Stylistics, and the Teaching of Composition*, edited by Donald A. McQuade, 123–41. Carbondale: Southern Illinois University Press.

Ferguson, Charles A. 1983. "Sports Announcer Talk." *Language in Society* 12: 155–73.

———. 1994. "Dialect, Register, and Genre: Working Assumptions about Conventionalization." In *Sociolinguistic Perspectives on Register*, edited by Douglas Biber and Edward Finegan. 15–30. Oxford Studies in Sociolinguistics, edited by Edward Finegan. Oxford, England: Oxford University Press.

Ferrara, Kathleen, Hans Brunner, and Greg Whittemore. 1991. "Interactive Written Discourse as an Emergent Register." *Written Communication* 8: 8–34.

Finholt, Tom, and Lee S. Sproull. 1990. "Electronic Groups at Work." *Organization Sciences* 1: 41–64.

Fleischman, Suzanne. 1990. "Philology, Linguistics, and the Discourse of the Medieval Text." *Speculum* 65: 19–37.

Foulger, Davis. 1990. "Medium as Process: The Structure, Use, and Practice of Computer Conferencing on IBM's IBMPC Computer Conferencing." Ph.D. Dissertation, Temple University.

Fromkin, Victoria, and Robert Rodman. 1993. *An Introduction to Language.* 5th ed. New York: Holt, Rinehart and Winston.

Galegher, Jolene, Robert Kraut, and Carmen Egido, eds. 1990. *Intellectual Teamwork: Social and Technological Foundations of Cooperative Work.* Hillsdale, N.J.: Lawrence Erlbaum.

Giles, Howard, Justine Coupland, and Nikolas Coupland. 1991. *Contexts of Accommodation: Developments in Applied Sociolinguistics.* Cambridge, England: Cambridge University Press.

Giles, Howard, and P. F. Powesland. 1975. *Speech Styles and Social Evaluation.* London, England, and New York: Academic Press.

Givón, Talmy, ed. 1983a. *Topic Continuity in Discourse: A Quantitative Cross-Language Study.* Amsterdam: John Benjamins.

———. 1983b. "Topic Continuity in Discourse: An Introduction." In *Topic Continuity in Discourse: A Quantitative Cross-Language Study*, 1–41. Amsterdam: John Benjamins.

Goodwin, Charles, and Marjorie H. Goodwin. 1992. "Assessments and the Construction of Context." In *Rethinking Context: Language as an Interactive Phenomenon*, edited by A. Duranti and Charles Goodwin, 147–91. Cambridge, England: Cambridge University Press.

Greenbaum, Sidney, and Randolph Quirk. 1990. *A Student's Grammar of the English Language.* London, England: Longman.

Grice, H. Paul. 1975. "Logic and Conversation." In *Speech Acts*, edited by Peter Cole and J. L. Morgan. Syntax and Semantics III: Speech Acts. Vol. 3. New York: Academic Press.

Grimes, Joseph E. 1975. *The Thread of Discourse.* Berlin, New York, Amsterdam: Mouton.

Grimshaw, Allen D., ed. 1990. *Conflict Talk: Sociolinguistic Investigations of Arguments in Conversations.* Cambridge, England: Cambridge University Press.

Gumperz, J. 1992. "Contextualization and Understanding." In *Rethinking Context: Language as an Interactive Phenomenon*, edited by Alesandro Duranti and Charles Goodwin, 229–52. Cambridge, England: Cambridge University Press.

Halliday, M. A. K. 1977. *Language as Social Semiotic*. Baltimore, MD: University Park Press.

———. 1985a. *An Introduction to Functional Grammar*. London, England: Edward Arnold.

———. 1985b. *Spoken and Written Language*. Geelong, Australia: Deakin University Press.

———. 1994. *An Introduction to Functional Gramar*. 2nd ed. London: Edward Arnold.

Halliday, M. A. K. and Ruqaiya Hasan. 1976. *Cohesion in English*. London, England: Longman.

Halliday, M. A. K., and J. R. Martin. 1993. *Writing Science: Literacy and Discursive Power*. Pittsburgh Series in Composition, Literacy, and Culture. Pittsburgh: University of Pittsburgh Press.

Hanks, William F. 1992. "The Indexical Ground of Deictic Reference." Chap. 2 In *Rethinking Context: Language as an Interactive Phenomenon*, edited by Alessandro Duranti and Charles Goodwin, 43–76. Studies in the Social and Cultural Foundations of Language. Cambridge, England: Cambridge University Press.

Harasim, Linda M., ed. 1990. *Online Education: Perspectives on a New Environment*. Foreword by Murray Turoff. New York: Praeger Publishers.

Harrison, Teresa M., and Timothy Stephen, eds. 1996a. *Computer Networking and Scholarly Communication in the Twenty-First-Century University*. Computer-Mediated Communication. Albany: State University of New York Press.

———. 1996b. "Computer Networking, Communication, and Scholarship." In *Computer Networking and Scholarly Communication in the Twenty-First-Century University*, edited by Teresa M. Harrison and Timothy Stephen, 3–36. Albany: State University of New York Press.

Hawisher, Gail and Paul LeBlanc, eds. 1992. *Re-Imaging Computers and Composition: Teaching and Research in the Virtual Age*. Portsmouth, NH: Boynton-Cook/Heinemann.

Herring, Susan C. 1993. "Gender and Democracy in Computer-Mediated Communication." *Electronic Journal of Communication* 3: no paging.

Hiltz, Starr Roxanne. 1984. *Online Communities: A Case Study of the Office of the Future*. Human/Computer Inteaction. Norwood, N.J.: Ablex.

Hiltz, Starr Roxanne, and Kenneth Johnson. 1989. "Experiments in Group Decision-Making, 3: Disinhibition, Deindividuation, and Group

Process in Pen Name and Real Name." *Decision Support Systems* 5: 217–32.

Holdstein, Deborah H., and Cynthia L. Selfe, eds. 1990. *Computers and Writing: Theory, Research, Practice*. New York: Modern Language Association of America.

Hopper, Paul J. 1987. "Emergent Grammar." In *Proceedings of the Thirteenth Annual Meeting of the Berkeley Linguistics Society*, edited by J. Aske, N. Beery, L. Michaels, and H. Filip, 139–57. Berkeley: University of California Press.

Hymes, Dell. 1972. "Models of the Interaction of Language and Social Life." In *Directions in Sociolinguistics*, edited by John J. Gumperz and Dell Hymes, 35–71. New York, NY: Holt, Rinehart, and Winston.

Ilie, Cornelia. 1994. *What Else Can I Tell You?: A Pragmatic Study of English Rhetorical Questions as Discursive and Argumentative Acts*. Stockholm Studies in English. Dissertation, University of Stockholm. Stockholm, Sweden: Almqvist & Wiksell International.

Jakobson, Roman. 1990. *On Language*. Cambridge, Mass.: Harvard University Press.

Jespersen, Otto. 1922. *Language: Its Nature, Development and Origin*. London, England: G. Allen & Unwin.

Johnstone, Barbara. 1990. *Stories, Community and Place: Narratives from Middle America*. Bloomington: Indiana University Press.

———. 1996. *The Linguistic Individual: Self-Expression in Language and Linguistics*. Oxford, England: Oxford University Press.

Jones, Linda Kay. 1977. *Theme in English Expository Discourse*. Edward Sapir Monograph Series in Language, Culture, and Cognition, edited by Adam Makkai and Valerie Becker Makkai, 2. Lake Bluff, Ill.: Jupiter Press.

Joos, Martin. 1967. *The Five Clocks*. Introduction by Albert H. Marckwardt. New York: Harcourt, Brace and World.

Kaye, Anthony, ed. 1992. *Collaborative Learning Through Computer Conferencing: The Najaden Papers*. Series F: Computer and Systems Sciences, 90. Berlin: Springer-Verlag.

Kertzer, Jonathan. 1989. *Poetic Argument: Studies in Modern Poetry*. Kingston, Ontario: McGill- Queen's University Press.

Labov, William. 1969. "Contraction, Deletion and Inherent Variability of the English Copula." *Language* 45: 715–62.

———. 1972. "The Transformation of Experience in Narrative Syntax." In *Language in the Inner City: Studies in the Black English Vernacular*, by William Labov, 354–396. Philadelphia: University of Pennsylvania Press.

Lanham, Richard A. 1992. "Digital Rhetoric: Theory, Practice, and Property." In *Literacy Online: The Promise (and Peril) of Reading and*

Writing with Computers, edited by Myron C. Tuman, 221–24. Pittsburgh: University of Pittsburgh Press.

———. 1993. *The Electronic Word: Democracy, Technology, and the Arts.* Chicago: University of Chicago Press.

Lehmann, Winfred P. 1962. *Historical Linguistics: An Introduction.* New York: Holt, Rinehart and Winston.

Levin, James A., Haesun Kim, and Margaret M. Riel. 1990. "Message Maps." In *Online Education: Perspectives on a New Environment,* edited by Linda M. Harasim. New York: Praeger Publishers.

Lucy, John A. 1993a. "Reflexive Language and the Human Disciplines." In *Reflexive Language: Reported Speech and Metapragmatics,* edited by John A. Lucy, 9–32. Cambridge, England: Cambridge University Press.

_____, ed. 1993b. *Reflexive Language: Reported Speech and Metapragmatics.* Cambridge, England: Cambridge University Press.

Lyons, John. 1977. *Semantics.* Cambridge, England, and New York: Cambridge University Press.

Mardh, Ingrid. 1980. "Headlinese: On the Grammar of English Front Page Headlines." *Lund Studies in English* 58.

Martin, J. R. 1992. *English Text: System and Structure.* Philadelphia: John Benjamins.

McGrath, Joseph E. 1990. "Time Matters in Groups." In *Intellectual Teamwork: Social and Technological Foundations of Cooperative Work,* edited by Jolene Galegher, Robert Kraut, and Carmen Egido, 23–62. Hillsdale, N.J.: Lawrence Erlbaum.

McQuade, Donald A., ed. 1986. *The Territory of Language: Linguistics, Stylistics, and the Teaching of Composition.* Carbondale: Southern Illinois University Press.

Metz, J. Michel. 1994. "Computer-Mediated Communication: Literature Review of a New Context." *Interpersonal Computing and Technology: An Electronic Journal for the 21st Century* 2: 31–49.

Michel, Kathleen. 1992. "Gender Differences in Computer-Mediated Conversations." *Kidlink.* Electronic address, http://www.kidlink.org/

Miller, J. Hillis. 1982. *Fiction and Repetition.* Cambridge, Mass.: Harvard University Press.

Milroy, Lesley. 1990. *Language and Social Networks.* London England: Basil Blackwell.

Moffett, James. 1965. "I, You, It." *College Composition and Communication* 16: 243–48.

Mühlhäusler, Peter and Rom Harré. 1990. *Pronouns and People: The Linguistic Construction of Social and Personal Identity.* Language in Society, edited by Peter Trudgill. With the assistance of Anthony Holiday and Michael Freyne. Oxford, UK: Blackwell.

Murray, Denise E. 1989. "When the Medium Determines Turns: Turn-Taking in Computer Conversation." In *Working with Language: A Multidisciplinary Consideration of Language Use in Work Contexts*, edited by Hywel Coleman. Contributions to the Sociology of Language, edited by Joshua A. Fishman. Berlin: Mouton de Gruyter.

―――. 1991. *Conversation for Action: the Computer Terminal as Medium of Communication*. Philadelphia: John Benjamins.

―――. 1995. *Knowledge Machines: Language and Information in a Technological Society*. Language in Social Life. New York: Longman.

Myers-Scotton, Carol. 1993a. *Duelling Languages: Grammatical Structure in Codeswitching*. Oxford, England: Clarendon Press.

―――. 1993b. *Social Motivations for Codeswitching: Evidence from Africa*. Oxford Studies in Language Contact. Oxford, England: Clarendon Press.

Ochs, Elinor. 1990. "Indexicality and Socialization." In *Cultural Psychology: Essays on Comparative Human Development*, edited by James W. Stigler, Richard A. Shweder, and Gilbert Hertdt, 287–308. Cambridge, England: Cambridge University Press.

―――. 1992. "Indexing Gender." In *Rethinking Context: Language as an Interactive Phenomenon*, edited by Alessandro Duranti and Charles Goodwin, 335–58. Studies in the Social and Cultural Foundations of Language. Cambridge, England: Cambridge University Press.

―――. 1994. "Stories That Step into the Future." In *Sociolinguistics of Register*, edited by Douglas Biber and Edward Finegan, 106–35. New York: Oxford University Press.

Ochs, Elinor, Carolyn Taylor, Dina Rudolph, and Ruth Smith. 1992. "Storytelling as a Theory-Building Activity." *Discourse Processes* 15: 37–72.

Palmer, F. R. 1986. *Mood and Modality*. Cambridge, England: Cambridge University Press.

―――. 1990. *Modality and the English Modals*. Longman Linguistics Library. 2nd ed. London, England, and New York: Longman.

Pinker, Steven. 1994. *The Language Instinct*. New York: William Morrow.

Prince, Gerald. 1980. "Introduction to the Study of the Narratee." In *Read-Response Criticism: From Formalism to Post-Structuralism*, edited by Jane P. Tompkins. Baltimore: Johns Hopkins University Press.

―――. 1983. "Narrative Pragmatics, Message, and Point." *Poetics* 12: 527–36.

―――. 1992. "Narratology, Narrative, and Meaning." *Poetics Today* 12: 543–52.

Purves, Alan C. 1990. *The Scribal Society: An Essay on Literacy and Schooling in the Information Age*. Photographs by Ted Purves. New York: Longman.

Quirk, Randolph, Sidney Greenbaum, Geoffrey Leech, and Jan Svartvik. 1972. *A Grammar of Contemporary English.* London: Longman.

———. 1985. *A Comprehensive Grammar of the English Language.* Index by David Crystal. London, England and New York, NY: Longman.

Rice, Ronald. 1980. "Computer Conferencing." In *Progress in Communication Sciences II*, edited by Brenda Dervin and Melvin Voight, 215–240. Norwood, NJ: Ablex.

———. 1982. "Communication Networking in Computer Conferencing Systems: A Longitudinal Study of Group Roles and System Structure." In *Communication Yearbook 6*, edited by Michael Burgoon, 925–44. Beverly Hills, Calif.: Sage.

———. "Computer-Mediated Communication and Organizational Innovation." *Journal of Communication* 37: 65–94.

Rice, Ronald and George Barnett. 1986. "Group Communication Networking in an Information Environment: Applying Metric Multidimensional Scaling." In *Communication Yearbook 9*, edited by Margaret McLaughlin, 315–338. Beverly Hills, Calif.: Sage.

Rieber, Robert W., and William A. Stewart, eds. 1990. *The Language Scientist as Expert in the Legal Setting.* Annals of the New York Academy of Sciences. 606.

Scherer, Laus, and Howard Giles, eds. 1979. *Social Markers in Speech.* Cambridge, England: Cambridge University Press.

Schiffrin, Deborah. 1987. *Discourse Markers.* Cambridge, England: Cambridge University Press.

———. 1990. "Management of a Co-operative Self During Argument." In *Conflict Talk: Sociolinguistic Investigations of Arguments in Conversations*, edited by Allen D. Grimshaw, 241–60. Cambridge, England: Cambridge University Press.

———. 1994. *Approaches to Discourse.* Blackwell Textbooks in Linguistics. Oxford, England, and Cambridge, Mass.: Blackwell.

Schwartz, Helen. 1992. "'Dominion Everywhere': Computers as Cultural Artifacts." In *Literacy Online: The Promise (and Peril) of Reading and Writing with Computers*, edited by Myron C. Tuman, 95–108. Pittsburgh: University of Pittsburgh Press.

Scollon, Ron, and Suzanne Wong Scollon. 1995. *Intercultural Communication.* Oxford, England: Basil Blackwell.

Selfe, Cynthia L., and Paul R. Meyer. 1991. "Testing Claims for Online Conferences." *Written Communication* 8: 163–92.

Shuy, Roger W. 1982. "Topic as the Unit of Analysis in a Criminal Law Case." In *Analyzing Discourse: Text and Talk*, edited by Deborah Tannen, 113–26. Washington, D.C.: Georgetown University Press.

———. 1984. "Entrapment and the Linguistics Analysis of Tapes." *Studies in Language* 8: 215–34.

————. 1990. "Evidence of Cooperation in Conversation: Topic-Type in a Solicitation to Murder Case." In *The Language Scientist as Expert in the Legal Setting: Issues in Forensic Linguistics*, edited by Robert W. Rieber and William A. Stewart, 85–105. Annals of the New York Academy of Sciences, 606.

Sidner, Candace. 1983. "Focusing and Discourse." *Discourse Processes* 6: 107–30.

Silverstein, Michael. 1976. "Shifters, Linguistic Categories, and Cultural Description." In *Meaning in Anthropology*, edited by Keith Basso and H. A. Selby, 11–56. Albuquerque: University of New Mexico Press.

Sproull, Lee, and Sara Kiesler. 1991. *Connections: New Ways of Working in the Networked Organization*. Cambridge, Mass.: MIT Press.

Straumann, H. 1935. *Newspaper Headlines: A Study in Linguistic Method*. London, England: Allen & Unwin.

Stubbs, Michael. 1996. *Text & Corpus Analysis: Computer-Assisted Studies of Language and Culture*. Language in Society. Oxford, England: Blackwell Publishers.

Svartvik, Jan, ed. 1992. *Directions in Corpus Linguistics: Proceedings of Nobel Symposium 82*. Trends in Linguistics: Studies and Monographs, 65. Nobel Symposium 82, Stockholm, 4–8 August 1991. Stockholm, Sweden: Mouton de Gruyter.

Swales, John M. 1990. *Genre Analysis: English in Academic and Research Settings*. Cambridge Applied Linguistics Series, edited by Michael H. Long and Jack C. Richards. Cambridge, England: Cambridge University Press.

Tannen, Deborah. 1987. "Repetition in Conversation, Towards a Poetics of Talk." *Language* 63: 574–605.

————. 1989. *Talking Voices: Repetition, Dialogue and Imagery in Conversational Discourse*. Studies in Interactional Sociolinguistics, edited by John J. Gumperz, 6. Cambridge, England: Cambridge University Press.

————. 1990. *You Just Don't Understand: Women and Men in Conversation*. New York: Ballantine Books.

————. 1993a. "Introduction." In *Framing in Discourse*, edited by Deborah Tannen, 3–13. New York: Oxford University Press.

————. 1993b. "What's in a Frame? Surface Evidence for Underlying Expectations." In *Framing in Discourse*, edited by Deborah Tannen, 14–56. New York: Oxford University Press.

Trenholm, Sarah. 1992. *Interpersonal Communication*. 2nd ed. London, England: Wadsworth.

Trudgill, Peter. 1986. *Dialects in Contact*. Oxford, England: Basil Blackwell.

Tuman, Myron C., ed. 1992a. *Literacy Online: The Promise (and Peril) of Reading and Writing with Computers.* Pittsburgh Series in Composition, Literacy, and Culture. Pittsburgh: University of Pittsburgh Press.

———. 1992b. *Word Perfect: Literacy in the Computer Age.* Pittsburgh Series in Composition, Literacy, and Culture. Pittsburgh: University of Pittsburgh Press.

Turkle, Sherry. 1984. *The Second Self: Computers and the Human Spirit.* New York: Simon and Schuster.

Ure, J. 1971. "Lexical Density and Register Differentiation." In *Applications of Linguistics,* edited by G. Perren and J. L. M. Trim, 443–52. Cambridge, England: Cambridge University Press.

van Dijk, Teun A., ed. 1985. *Discourse Analysis in Society.* Handbook of Discourse Analysis, 4. Amsterdam: Academic Press.

van Dijk, Teun A., and Walter Kintsch, eds. 1983. *Strategies of Discourse Comprehension.* New York: Academic Press.

Watkins, Calvert. 1989. "New Parameters in Historical Linguistics, Philology, and Culture History." *Language* 65: 783–99.

———. 1990. "What is Philology?" *Comparative Literature Studies* 27: 21–25.

Wilkins, Harriet. 1991. "Long Distance Conversations by Computer." *Written Communication* 8: 56–98.

Winograd, Terry, and Fernando Flores. 1986. *Understanding Computers and Cognition.* Language and Being. Norwood, N.J.: Ablex.

Witte, Stephen P., and Roger D. Cherry. 1986. "Writing Processes and Written Products in Composition Research." In *Studying Writing: Linguistic Approaches,* edited by C. R. Cooper and Sidney Greenbaum, 112–54. Beverly Hills, CA: Sage.

Wittig, Rob. 1994. *Invisible Rendezvous: Connection and Collaboration in the New Landscape of Electronic Writing.* Hanover, N.H.: University Press of New England.

Wolfram, Walt. 1994. "On the Sociolinguistic Significance of Obscure Dialect Structures: The [NP$_i$ *call* NP$_i$ V-*ing*] Construction in African-American Vernacular English." *American Speech* 69: 339–60.

Wolfram, Walt. 1996. "Delineation and Description in Dialectology: The Case of Perfective *I'm* in Lumbee English." *American Speech* 71: 5–26.

Yancey, Kathleen Blake. 1994. *Voices on Voice: Perspectives, Definitions, Inquiry.* Urbana, Ill.: National Council of Teachers of English.

Youmans, Gilbert. 1991. "A New Tool for Discourse Analysis." *Language* 67: 763–789.

Zuboff, Shoshana. 1988. *The Age of the Smart Machine: The Future of Work and Power.* New York: Basic Books.

Index